50 DAYS OF PROSPERITY
Volume 2

by Pastor George Pearsons

"He will spend his days in prosperity and
his descendants will inherit the land."
Psalm 25:13, NIV

For more information about Kenneth Copeland Ministries, visit kcm.org or call 1-800-600-7395 (U.S. only) or +1-817-852-6000.

ISBN 978-1-60463-240-8
30-0825

Unless otherwise noted, all scripture is from the *King James Version* of the Bible.

Scripture quotations marked AMP are from *The Amplified Bible, Old Testament* © 1965, 1987 by the Zondervan Corporation. *The Amplified New Testament* © 1958, 1987 by The Lockman Foundation. Used by permission.

Scripture quotations marked NKJV are from the *New King James Version* © 1982 by Thomas Nelson Inc.

Scripture quotations marked NIV and NIV-84 are from *The Holy Bible, New International Version* © 1973, 1978, 1984, 2011 by Biblica, Inc. Used by permission. All rights reserved worldwide.

Scripture quotations marked NLT and NLT-96 are from the *Holy Bible, New Living Translation* © 1996, 2004 by Tyndale Charitable Trust. Used by permission of Tyndale House Publishers.

Scripture quotations marked MSG are from *The Message,* © 1993, 1994, 1995, 1996, 2000, 2001, 2002. Used by permission of NavPress Publishing Group.

Scripture quotations marked GW are from *God's Word,* a work of God's Word to the Nations, © 1995 by God's Word to the Nations. Quotations are used by permission.

Scripture quotations marked BBE are from the *Bible in Basic English,* public domain.

Scripture quotations marked DRB are from the *1899 Douay-Rheims Bible,* public domain.

Scripture quotations marked TLB are from *The Living Bible,* copyright © 1971. Used by permission of Tyndale House Publishers, Inc., Wheaton, Illinois 60189. All rights reserved.

Scripture quotations marked NRSV are from the *New Revised Standard Version Bible*, copyright 1989, Division of Christian Education of the National Council of the Churches of Christ in the United States of America. Used by permission. All rights reserved.

Scripture quotations marked GNB are taken from the Good News Bible—Second Edition © 1992 by American Bible Society. Used by permission.

Scripture quotations marked WNT are from *The New Testament in Modern Speech* by Richard Francis Weymouth © 1996 Kenneth Copeland Publications.

Scripture quotations marked CEV are from the *Contemporary English Version* © 1991, 1992, 1995 by American Bible Society. Used by Permission.

Scripture quotations marked WUEST are from *The New Testament: An Expanded Translation,* by Kenneth S. Wuest, © 1961 by Wm. B. Eerdmans Publishing. All rights reserved.

Scripture quotations marked KNOX are from *The Holy Bible: A Translation From the Latin Vulgate in the Light of the Hebrew and Greet Originals by Monsignor Ronald Knox.* © 1954 by Sheed & Ward, Inc., New York, with the kind permission of His Eminence, The Cardinal Archbishop of Westminster, and Burns and Oates, Ltd., 115 E. Armour Blvd., Kansas City, MO 64111.

Scripture quotations marked TCNT are from the *Twentieth Century New Testament*, public domain.

Quotations from *The Chumash, Stone Edition,* are from Rabbi Nosson Scherman, *The Chumash,* Vol. 1: Bereishis/Genesis, Personal Size Edition, Artscroll Series, Stone Edition (New York: Mesorah Publications Ltd.)

References to "Are You Prepared for Prosperity?" are excerpted from "The Kingdom Is at Hand" prophecy delivered by Kenneth Copeland on June 17, 2011, at the 2011 Annual Word of Faith Convention, Southfield, Mich. © 2011 Kenneth Copeland. All rights reserved.

References to the "God's Great Storehouse" prophecy are taken from the "What About 2012" prophecy, © 2011 Kenneth Copeland. All rights reserved.

Day #55
Quote from Kenneth Copeland, *THE BLESSING of The LORD Makes Rich and He Adds No Sorrow With It Proverbs 10:22* (Fort Worth: Kenneth Copeland Publications, 2011), page 125.

Day #64
Kenneth E. Hagin, from a 1999 Family Meeting in Tulsa, OK. Used with permission. For additional teaching on this subject, see Kenneth E. Hagin's minibook *How God Taught Me About Prosperity* and his book *Biblical Keys to Financial Prosperity.* www.rhema.org.

Day #65
Quotes from Kenneth Copeland, Kenneth and Gloria Copeland, *From Faith to Faith—A Daily Guide to Victory* (Fort Worth: Kenneth Copeland Publications, 1992), July 9 devotion.

Day #68
Quotes from Kenneth Copeland, Kenneth and Gloria Copeland, *From Faith to Faith—A Daily Guide to Victory* (Fort Worth: Kenneth Copeland Publications, 1992), November 13 devotion.

Day #69
Quotes from Gloria Copeland, *Blessed Beyond Measure—Experiencing the Extraordinary Goodness of God* (New York: Faith Words, 2008), pages 16-17.

Day #71:
Quotation from *The Chumash, Stone Edition,* are from Rabbi Nosson Scherman, *The Chumash,* Vol. 1: Bereishis/Genesis, Personal Size Edition, Artscroll Series, Stone Edition (New York: Mesorah Publications Ltd.), page 1077

Day #75
Quote from Kenneth Copeland, Kenneth and Gloria Copeland, *From Faith to Faith—A Daily Guide to Victory,* (Fort Worth: Kenneth Copeland Publications, 1992) August 12 devotion, "A Supernatural Cycle of Blessing"
Quote from Gloria Copeland, *The Kingdom of God—Days of Heaven on Earth*, message 4, "Your Heavenly Account, Part 1" © 1996

Day #76
Quote from Kenneth Copeland, *Living in Prosperity,* message 6, "Prosperity in Abundance" © 1982
Quote from Gloria Copeland, *The Kingdom of God—Days of Heaven on Earth*, message 4, "Your Heavenly Account, Part 1" © 1996

Day #77
Quote from Kenneth Copeland, *Living in Prosperity,* message 6, "Prosperity in Abundance" © 1982

Day #78
Quotes from *The Tehillim, ArtScroll Tanach Series,* Volume 1, Psalm 23, (Mesorah Publications, LTD), pages 288-289

Day #81:
Word from the Lord to Kenneth E. Hagin, *How You Can Be Led by the Spirit of God* (Tulsa, Okla., Faith Library Publications, 2004 Edition), page 25.
Quotes from Kenneth Copeland, *The Laws of Prosperity* (Fort Worth: Kenneth Copeland Publications, 1974) pages 22-23.
Excerpt from Kenneth Copeland, *Blessed to Be a Blessing—Understanding True, Biblical Prosperity* (Fort Worth: Kenneth Copeland Publications, 1997) page 5.
Page from Kenneth Copeland, Kenneth and Gloria Copeland, *From Faith to Faith—A Daily Guide to Victory,* (Fort Worth: Kenneth Copeland Publications, 1992) December 5 devotion.

Day #82:
Quote from Kenneth Copeland, Kenneth and Gloria Copeland, *True Prosperity,* © 2003.

Day #84
Excerpt from Kenneth Copeland, *Blessed to Be a Blessing—Understanding True, Biblical Prosperity* (Fort Worth: Kenneth Copeland Publications, 1997) page 122.
Quote from Gloria Copeland, *The Kingdom of God—Days of Heaven on Earth,* message 4, "Your Heavenly Account, Part 1" © 1996.

Day #85
Quote from Gloria Copeland, *The Kingdom of God—Days of Heaven on Earth,* message 4, "Your Heavenly Account, Part 1" © 1996.

Day #87
Quote from Gloria Copeland, *True Prosperity,* "Seven Things That Bring Increase, Part 2" © 2003.

Day #92
Quote by Gloria Copeland, *God's Will for You, Expanded Legacy Edition* (Fort Worth, Kenneth Copeland Publications, 1972, 2012), page 47.

Day #93
Quote from *Mishlei/Proverbs Volume 1, The ArtScroll Tanach Series,* (New York: Mesorah Publications Ltd.), page 241.
Quote from Gloria Copeland, *The Kingdom of God—Days of Heaven on Earth,* message 5, "Your Heavenly Account, Part 2" © 1996.

Day #94
Quote from Gloria Copeland, *True Prosperity,* "Seven Things That Bring Increase, Part 2" © 2003.
Quote from Gloria Copeland, *The Kingdom of God—Days of Heaven on Earth,* message 5, "Your Heavenly Account, Part 2" © 1996.

Day #96
Quotes from *The Tehillim, The ArtScroll Tanach Series,* 2-Volume Edition, Psalm 105, (Mesorah Publications, LTD), page 1283.

Day #97
Quote from Gloria Copeland, *The Kingdom of God—Days of Heaven on Earth,* message 5, "Your Heavenly Account, Part 2" © 1996.

Day #99
Quotes from Bill Winston, *Supernatural Wealth Transfer,* © 2012.

Day #100
Quotes from Gloria Copeland, *God's Will Is Prosperity* (Fort Worth, Kenneth Copeland Publications, 1978), pages 71-72, 89.

Dear Prosperous Believer,

Welcome to *50 Days of Prosperity—Volume 2*.

What began as a two-week prosperity series on the *Believer's Voice of Victory* broadcast has now blossomed into 100 days! You are holding the second set of 50 lessons focused on the laws of prosperity.

When Gloria Copeland and I began taping some of the earlier broadcasts, I said, "Gloria, you just can't exhaust the subject of prosperity." She immediately responded by saying, "Let's try!"

Teaching these lessons with Gloria has truly become a highlight of my life. She laughingly says that I do all the work by preparing these messages. "That way," she says, "all I have to do is come to the studio and let Pastor George do the work." Don't let her fool you. "All the work" has already been completed over the many, many, many years of solid and faithful teaching by the Copelands.

I gladly confess to you that the lion's share of this material has come straight from Kenneth and Gloria Copeland. My life was transformed by their ministry ever since I began dating my future wife, Terri Copeland, at Oral Roberts University in 1975. Terri was the one who introduced me to her dad's preaching. Wow! Once I heard my first life-altering message by Brother Copeland called *The Image of God in You,* I was hooked! Then, after listening to Gloria, I was double-hooked! Their solid stand of faith on God's Word has been an anchor ever since.

Gloria Copeland is woman of great wisdom. After I prepare the outlines (which have been researched by utilizing their books, their CDs and my own private collection of notes made over the years), Gloria always has something significant to add to what I have already written. That is why we have a "scribe" in attendance during tape days, in order to capture any revelations that she might have. After she shares those heavyweight nuggets, we add them to the outlines before they are released. We never forget that she is the teacher and we are the students!

Kenneth and Gloria have taught me the importance of giving God's Word first place and making it final authority in my life. So, when it comes to the study of any subject, including prosperity, God's Word is of primary importance. The more we saturate ourselves in the Word, the greater results we will see. Brother Copeland calls it "The Principle of Total Immersion."

"Total Immersion" is the reason for the format of these lessons. They will help you further develop your faith in God's determination to see you prosper.

With this ministry tool, you can watch the broadcasts and follow right along with the outlines. You have the benefit of having all the scriptures and the main thoughts that we discuss. You can stop and start as the Lord gives you further insights. Use these outlines as an opportunity for you and your family to immerse yourselves in a daily study of prosperity. As the Lord told Gloria many years ago, *In consistency lies the power.*

Since the release notes (both Volume 1 and the individual weeks), we have received tremendous reports from folks around the world as to how these lessons have changed their lives. Pastors are using them in their churches as extended studies with their congregations. One pastor wrote and said that he was using them as a children's curriculum! He decided to train them up in the way they should go!

Don't ever forget that it is God's will for you to prosper.

It is good to know that God loves us and passionately desires to prosper us. Psalm 35:27 says, "Let them shout for joy, and be glad, that favour my righteous cause: yea, let them say continually, Let the Lord be magnified, which hath pleasure in the prosperity of his servant."

It has always been the heart of our loving Father to take good care of His children. "Fear not, little flock," Luke 12:32 declares, "for it is your Father's good pleasure to give you the kingdom." He takes joy in supplying every need, removing every burden and watching us become a major blessing to others. As I have told my congregation many times here at Eagle Mountain International Church, "Our motivation for accumulation is distribution."

That is the heart of prosperity.

And that is the heart of Kenneth Copeland Ministries.

All of us here want you to prosper and be in good health, even as your soul prospers (3 John 2). But, it will take the renewing of your mind to God's way of prosperous thinking to step up to a new realm of believing and receiving. I have no doubt that you can—and will move up to the next level of prosperity. Now, get with the program and get immersed in God's Word. The result of this study is found in Psalm 115:14. "The Lord shall increase you more and more, you and your children."

Increasing more and more with you,

Pastor George Pearsons

DAYS OF PROSPERITY *Vol. 2*
Pastor George Pearsons

Table of Contents

DAYS OF PROSPERITY *Vol. 2*
Pastor George Pearsons

A Kingdom Transfer
Day #51

A. Colossians 1:12-14—Transferred From One Kingdom to Another
1. Verses 13-14 (NLT): "He has rescued us from the kingdom of darkness and transferred us into the Kingdom of his dear Son, who purchased our freedom and forgave our sins."
   a. Some translations add, "with His blood."
   b. AMP: "The Father has delivered and drawn us to Himself out of the control and the dominion of darkness and has transferred us into the kingdom of the Son of His love."
2. 1 Peter 2:9-10: "But ye are a chosen generation, a royal priesthood, an holy nation, a peculiar people; that ye should shew forth the praises of him who hath called you out of darkness into his marvellous light; which in time past were not a people, but are now the people of God: which had not obtained mercy, but now have obtained mercy."
   a. Darkness is lack, poverty and shortage.
   b. Darkness is a manifestation of the curse.
3. We no longer live under the dominion, rule and control of the kingdom of darkness.

B. John 17:14-17—Jesus Separated Us From Evil and the World's Failing System
1. Matthew 6:13: "And lead us not into temptation, but deliver us from evil: For thine is the kingdom, and the power, and the glory, for ever. Amen."
2. Galatians 1:3-4: "Grace be to you and peace from God the Father, and from our Lord Jesus Christ, who gave himself for our sins, that he might deliver us from this present evil world, according to the will of God and our Father."
   a. Verse 4 (AMP): "Who gave (yielded) Himself up [to atone] for our sins [and to save and sanctify us], in order to rescue and deliver us from this present wicked age and world order, in accordance with the will and purpose and plan of our God and Father."
3. 2 Peter 1:3-4 (AMP): Through God's promises, we have escaped "[by flight] from the moral decay (rottenness and corruption) that is in the world because of covetousness (lust and greed), and become sharers (partakers) of the divine nature."

C. Galatians 3:13-14—Jesus Separated Us From the Curse of Poverty and Lack
1. We have been redeemed from the curse of poverty and lack—which is darkness.
2. We may be in this world, but we are not of its Babylonian system.
3. We now operate under a new kingdom and a new economy.
4. We are not subject to the times. The times are subject to us.
5. We don't just survive in God's kingdom—we thrive!
   a. We live independent of circumstances.
   b. We live in THE BLESSING of kingdom prosperity.

West Coast Believers' Convention
Long Beach, California
July 2008

Give forth praise and honor, for The LORD says it is not time for the United States to fail. It is not time for this nation to collapse financially, or fold up spiritually, or go the way of the rest of the world, or the way that the rest of the world is trying to drag it and make it go.

It is time, right now, for this nation's greatest hour, its greatest outpouring, and its greatest financial blessing. It's My time, says The LORD Jesus Christ. We will see it come to pass. You mark My words.

DAYS OF PROSPERITY *Vol. 2*
Pastor George Pearsons

Seek First the Kingdom
Day #52

A. Matthew 6:33—Seek First the Kingdom of God
1. AMP: "Seek, (aim at and strive after) first of all His kingdom and His righteousness (His way of doing and being right), and then all these things taken together will be given you besides."
   a. We seek the kingdom of God by putting God's Word first place in our lives.
   b. God's Word is final authority in His kingdom.
2. Everything that we need in life has already been given to us.
3. 2 Peter 1:3: "According as his divine power hath given unto us all things that pertain unto life and godliness, through the knowledge of him that hath called us to glory and virtue."
   a. AMP: "For His divine power has bestowed upon us all things that [are requisite and suited] to life and godliness, through the [full, personal] knowledge of Him Who called us by and to His own glory and excellence (virtue)."
   b. NLT: "By his divine power, God has given us everything we need for living a godly life."

B. Philippians 4:19—The Kingdom of God Is Our Source of Supply
1. AMP: "And my God will liberally supply (fill to the full) your every need according to His riches in glory in Christ Jesus."
   a. BBE: "My God will give you all you have need of from the wealth of his glory."
2. We are separated from the kingdom of darkness and are now governed by a new kingdom and a new economy.
3. We don't just survive in the kingdom of God—we thrive!

C. The Results of Seeking God's Kingdom
1. 2 Chronicles 26:5: "As long as [Uzziah] sought the Lord, God made him to prosper."
   a. *Sought* (HEB) = Diligently inquire, research, investigate, consult
2. Psalm 34:8-10: "O taste and see that the Lord is good: blessed is the man that trusteth in him. O fear the Lord, ye his saints: for there is no want to them that fear him. The young lions do lack, and suffer hunger: but they that seek the Lord shall not want any good thing."
   a. GW: "Those who seek the Lord's help will have all the good things they need."
   b. DRB: "…shall not be deprived."

3. Proverbs 8:17-21 (TLB): "I love all who love me. Those who search for me shall surely find me. Unending riches, honor, justice and righteousness are mine to distribute. My gifts are better than the purest gold or sterling silver! My paths are those of justice and right. Those who love and follow me are indeed wealthy. I fill their treasuries."

EAGLE MOUNTAIN
International Church

DAYS OF PROSPERITY *Vol. 2*
Pastor George Pearsons

Always Plenty in the Kingdom
Day #53

A. Genesis 26—A Kingdom Man in Tough Times
1. Isaac is the picture of a kingdom man who flourished during a serious economic downturn.
2. He may have been *in* the famine—but he remained untouched *by* the famine.
3. This account is an example of how we should thrive and flourish in the kingdom of God in spite of the economy.

B. Genesis 26:1—There Was a Famine in the Land
1. MSG: "There was a famine in the land, as bad as the famine during the time of Abraham."
2. Genesis 12:10: "And there was a famine in the land: and Abram went down into Egypt to sojourn there; for the famine was grievous in the land."
   a. NIV—The famine was severe.
   b. MSG—It was a hard famine.
   c. AMP—It was oppressive, intense and grievous.
3. *Famine* defined.
   a. Severe shortage of everything
   b. Extreme scarcity
   c. Serious economic downturn
   d. To be left wanting
   e. To fall short

C. Jeremiah 17:5-8—There Is Always Plenty in the Kingdom of God
1. Even during an economic downturn
2. Verse 8 (NLT): "They are like trees planted along a riverbank, with roots that reach deep into the water. Such trees are not bothered by the heat or worried by long months of drought. Their leaves stay green and they never stop producing fruit."
   a. *Green* (HEB) = Flourish, prosper, thrive
3. Psalm 92:12: "The righteous shall flourish like the palm tree."
4. We are not subject to the economy—the economy is subject to THE BLESSING of the kingdom.
5. We are here to carry THE BLESSING of kingdom prosperity wherever we go.

DAYS OF PROSPERITY *Vol. 2*
Pastor George Pearsons

Thriving in Times of Famine

Day #54

A. Genesis 26:1—There Was a Famine in the Land
1. Severe shortage of everything
2. Extreme scarcity
3. Serious economic downturn
4. To be left wanting
5. To fall short

B. What God's Word Tells Us About Living in Times of Famine
1. Job 5:20, 22: "In famine he shall redeem thee from death…. At destruction and famine thou shalt laugh."
2. Psalm 33:18-19: "The eye of the Lord is upon them that fear him, upon them that hope in his mercy [NLT—rely on his unfailing love]; to deliver their soul from death, and to keep them alive in famine."
   a. MSG: "God's eye is on those who respect him, the ones who are looking for his love. He's ready to come to their rescue in bad times; in lean times he keeps body and soul together."
   b. We are depending on God. He is everything we need.
3. Psalm 37:18-19: "The Lord knoweth the days of the upright: and their inheritance shall be for ever. They shall not be ashamed in the evil time: and in the days of famine they shall be satisfied."
   a. *Satisfied* (HEB) = To have enough, to be filled up, to have plenty of
   b. NLT: "They will not be disgraced in hard times; even in famine they will have more than enough."
   c. NIV: "In times of disaster they will not wither; in days of famine they will enjoy plenty."
   d. HEB—He will supply until no more is needed.
4. Romans 8:35, 37: "Who shall separate us from the love of Christ? shall tribulation, or distress, or persecution, or famine, or nakedness, or peril, or sword?... Nay, in all these things we are more than conquerors through him that loved us."
5. "Wherever we go, the kingdom of God goes." —Gloria Copeland

C. Proverbs 10:22—"THE BLESSING of the Lord, it maketh rich, and He addeth no sorrow with it."
1. In times of famine, we don't just survive—WE THRIVE!
2. *Thrive*—prosper, flourish, succeed, advance, grow vigorously, increase in goods and estates
3. In spite of the economy
4. We are to follow the Genesis 1:28 example.
5. Be fruitful, multiply, replenish, subdue and have dominion over

"A Feast of Abundance in the Valley of the Shadow of Death"

Word From the Lord Through Kenneth Copeland
Southwest Believers' Convention
August 7, 2009

I have plans that you have never dreamed of, saith The LORD. They are beyond your wildest imagination. I did it just for you.

Heaven is overloaded with things that I have prepared for your enjoyment, if you will simply come to that place where you just say, "God, I am so grateful," and give Me an opportunity.

Become a giver and not a taker.

Become a thinker like I think.

I will think through your mind. I will see through your eyes. I will speak through your lips. I will give you power within that is far greater than anything you have ever imagined.

I need you to help Me in these end times to raise up an army of believers. And you are my key personnel. I don't need you broke! I don't need you sick! I need you healed and well! I paid for it! Come and get it! Come and dine! Come and dine! Come to the table! I have prepared a table in the presence of your enemies.

This is not a heavenly feast. You don't have any enemies in heaven!

This is a feast of abundance in the valley of the shadow of death.

Fear no evil! Fear not the shadow of death nor the valley therein. I am your LORD and your Savior. I am The LORD of Hosts, and I am the biggest thing in the valley.

Have no fear, for the table is full. Come and dine. Come and dine. Pass the healing. Pass the debt-free pudding. Pass the miracles down here on this end of the table. Come and dine. Come and dine.

I will send you to places and I will anoint you, and I will take care of you while you are there. And people will be amazed at the grace that comes out of your mouth and the riches that come through your hands.

Whole nations will come to Me.

Trillions are nothing to Me.

747s are nothing to Me. All things were created for and by Me, saith The LORD, and I don't need your airplanes up here. My chariot way outclasses that. Have you not seen in My WORD where My chariot is like the lightning from the east to the west? My stuff moves at the speed of light. Your stuff is extremely slow. But stay with Me, and you will get faster.

DAYS OF PROSPERITY *Vol. 2*
Pastor George Pearsons

Obedience and Prosperity

Day #55

A. Genesis 26:2-6—Isaac Obeyed God in Famine
1. "Do not descend to Egypt, for you are an unblemished offering and it does not befit you to reside outside the land." *(The Chumash, The Stone Edition)*
2. Verses 3-4—Isaac prospered right where he was.
    a. God needed Isaac there to establish the Garden of Eden.
    b. God needs us here to establish the Garden of Eden.
3. Verse 3-5—The result of obedience.
    a. *Sojourn*—take possession because you own the place.
    b. The land was his, promised in the Abrahamic Covenant.
    c. "If you will walk around with the attitude of faith, I will do for you exactly what I did for your father. I will give you everything I gave him." —Kenneth Copeland, *THE BLESSING of The LORD Makes Rich and He Adds No Sorrow With It*
4. Verse 6—Isaac obeyed and stayed in Gerar.
5. "Don't go to the world—go to the Word." —Gloria Copeland

B. Genesis 26:3-6—Obedience Opens the Door to Kingdom Prosperity
1. Isaiah 1:19: "If ye be willing and obedient, ye shall eat the good of the land."
    a. NLT: "…You will eat the best of the land."
    b. MSG: "If you'll willingly obey, you'll feast like kings."
    c. Your prosperity is on the other side of your obedience.
2. Job 36:11: "If they obey and serve him, they shall spend their days in prosperity, and their years in pleasures."
    a. *Pleasures* (HEB) = Your years will be delightful, pleasant and sweet.
    b. NLT: "If they listen and obey God, they will be blessed with prosperity throughout their lives."
    c. NIV: "If they obey and serve him, they will spend the rest of their days in prosperity and their years in contentment."
3. Deuteronomy 28:1-2 (NLT): "If you fully obey the Lord your God and carefully keep all his commands that I am giving you today, the Lord your God will set you high above all the nations of the world. You will experience all these blessings if you obey the Lord your God."
    a. KJV: "And all these blessings shall come on thee and overtake thee."

b. NIV: "All these blessings will come on you and accompany you if you obey the Lord your God."

c. *Overtake*—Engulf you, pile up on you, swamp, flood, overflow, heap, cover

C. A Conversation Between Kenneth Copeland and Pastor George Pearsons, April 19, 1997

"Obedience in Sowing KCM's First Airplane"

The first airplane that Kenneth and Gloria Copeland sowed was in 1972. It was a 1959 Cessna 310. Kenneth and Gloria were believing for a larger airplane as well as an additional $50,000 for a television ministry project.

One day while driving, Brother Copeland asked the Lord, "How will I ever be able to get a new airplane AND do this television project?"

The Lord said, *You know exactly how to do that. Luke 6:38 says, "Give, and it shall be given unto you; good measure, pressed down, and shaken together, and running over, shall men give into your bosom. For with the same measure that ye mete withal it shall be measured to you again."*

Later, during a meeting, he and Jerry Savelle agreed get up at 5:00 each morning to pray about this situation. God confirmed to them exactly what to do—and Brother Copeland immediately obeyed.

He and Gloria sowed their Cessna 310 into another ministry. At the time, the plane's worth was $25,000—3/4 of the assets of the Kenneth Copeland Evangelistic Association.

Ten days later, a woman walked into the Copelands' office. She excitedly declared that she had a miracle take place with some stock.

She presented Brother Copeland with a check for $250,000.

They bought a Cessna 414 and moved ahead with their television project.

Brother Copeland then told me, "We have never been without since. We didn't just confess a little every now and then. The thought of talking lack around each other became profanity. Once the seed is sown, you must become so totally committed that you never yield. 'What if we don't have enough? So what!' After you have sown and received, the question becomes, 'Will you settle for what you have, or will you sow it for more?' Do not get in fear and settle for what you have gained. Sow for more!"

Update: As of Sept. 1, 2011, Kenneth Copeland Ministries has sown 22 airplanes into other ministries. KCM has also contributed money toward the purchase of eight aircraft to other ministries.

From the Book
THE BLESSING of The LORD Makes Rich and He Adds No Sorrow With It
by Kenneth Copeland

If we'll just believe what the Bible says about us and walk in the covenant of love, THE BLESSING will produce the conditions of the Garden of Eden around us as surely as it did for the Israelites in the Promised Land. In fact, it will do even more for us than it did for them. Because we carry THE BLESSING inside us wherever we go, God can send us to the hardest, thistle-growing, demon-infested place, and we can go with joy. We don't have to argue with Him about it. We don't have to complain and drag our feet. We can go in faith knowing that God is sending us there not to live in squalor but to release THE BLESSING that's within us and turn that dark corner of the world into a milk-and-honey kind of place.

"Oh, Brother Copeland, you're not being practical. There are some places even THE BLESSING won't work."

If there are, I've never seen them, and I've been to a lot of places. I've seen THE BLESSING work everywhere from the wilds of Africa to the urban jungles of America....

EAGLE MOUNTAIN
International Church

DAYS OF PROSPERITY *Vol. 2*
Pastor George Pearsons

Sowing in Famine

Day #56

A. Ecclesiastes 11:4—"Maybe It's Not a Good Time to Sow"
1. AMP: "He who observes the wind [and waits for all conditions to be favorable] will not sow, and he who regards the clouds will not reap."
2. NLT: "Farmers who wait for perfect weather never plant. If they watch every cloud, they never harvest."
3. It is always a good time to sow in the kingdom of God.
    a. Luke 6:38: "Give and it shall be given unto you."
    b. 2 Corinthians 9:6—He which sows bountifully shall reap also bountifully.

B. Genesis 26:12—Isaac Sowed in Famine
1. NIV: "Isaac planted crops in that land and the same year reaped a hundredfold because the Lord blessed him."
2. "His crop was a hundred times as much as the expected estimate. According to our Rabbis, Isaac was scrupulous to determine the quantity of the crop in order to establish how much he was required to give tithes (Rashi)." —*The Chumash, The Stone Edition*
3. A hundredfold return was an unusual harvest for Gerar.
    a. Even in more fertile regions, the yield was usually not greater than twenty-five- to fiftyfold.
    b. This was a kingdom harvest in a time of famine.
    c. Two testimonies
        i. The family in Oklahoma whose garden produced in time of drought
        ii. The 14forty Watermelon Miracle (see attachment)
4. Jeremiah 17:7-8—We harvest in spite of the conditions.
    a. NLT: "Blessed are those who trust in the Lord and have made the Lord their hope and confidence. They are like trees planted along a riverbank, with roots that reach deep into the water. Such trees are not bothered by the heat or worried by long months of drought. Their leaves stay green, and they never stop producing fruit."
    b. "Her leaf shall be green; and shall not be careful in the year of drought, neither shall cease from yielding fruit."
5. We harvest continual prosperity even during the toughest times.

C. Mark 10:29-30—The Hundredfold Return

    1. "But he shall receive an hundredfold now in this time."

    2. Luke 18:30: "Who shall not receive manifold more in this present time."

        a. MSG: "It will all come back multiplied many times over in your lifetime. And then the bonus of eternal life!"

        b. NRSV—You will receive much more in this age.

    3. "The hundredfold return is working for me all the time."

The 14Forty Watermelon Miracle

At the end of every school year, EMIC's 14forty youth group has a "School's Out Party." The party two years ago included watermelon and volleyball. Little did they know that this party would become a lesson on seedtime and harvest!

They began noticing something unusual in the volleyball court sometime after the party. It appeared that the students had been spitting out the watermelon seeds as they sat and watched the volleyball games. Over time, the seeds began to sprout and little watermelons appeared. Isaiah 55:10-11 (NLT) became a reality. "The rain and snow come down from the heavens and stay on the ground to water the earth. They cause the grain to grow, producing seed for the farmer and bread for the hungry. It is the same with my word. I send it out, and it always produces fruit. It will accomplish all I want it to, and it will prosper everywhere I send it."

This past spring, the youth group leaders requested the KCM maintenance department to clean up the volleyball court for summer use. The standard procedure included spraying chemicals to destroy the weeds. The request was fulfilled. However, in spite of the chemicals plus the summer drought, the watermelons returned! It was a supernatural harvest of THE BLESSING. The Lord supplied the seed, and the Lord produced the harvest.

And, by the fruit of their lips, the students were the vessels!

DAYS OF PROSPERITY *Vol. 2*
Pastor George Pearsons

Kingdom Increase
Day #57

A. Genesis 26:13-14—Increase in Times of Famine
  1. "The man waxed great, and went forward, and grew until he became very great: For he had possession of flocks, and possession of herds, and great store of servants: and the Philistines envied him."
      a. *Wax great* (HEB) = To prosper, increase, advance, enlarge and expand
      b. *He became very great* (HEB) = Speedily, rapidly, quickly
      c. "The man (Yitzchak) became prosperous, and he grew constantly great until he had grown very great (even in comparison to Abimelech)." —The Chumash, The Stone Edition
  2. Because of THE BLESSING, Isaac quickly prospered, increased, advanced and expanded—all during an economic downturn.
  3. Translations
      a. NKJV: "The man began to prosper, and continued prospering until he became very prosperous; for he had possessions of flocks and possessions of herds and a great number of servants. So the Philistines envied him."
      b. NLT: "He became a very rich man, and his wealth continued to grow [NIV: "until he became very wealthy"]. He acquired so many flocks of sheep and goats, herds of cattle, and servants that the Philistines became jealous of him."
      c. AMP: "And the man became great and gained more and more until he became very wealthy and distinguished; he owned flocks, herds, and a great supply of servants, and the Philistines envied him."
      d. MSG: "The man got richer and richer by the day until he was very wealthy."
      e. "He had flocks of sheep and cattle and many enterprises." —*The Chumash, The Stone Edition*

B. Genesis 26:14-16—The Philistines' Jealousy
  1. Jealousy comes as a result of wanting what someone else has.
      a. People are not jealous over the lack of another.
      b. They become jealous over another's increase and success.
  2. Isaac became the richest man in the world.
      a. Isaac's home became bigger than Abimelech's palace.
      b. Isaac's staff, riches and estate increased in the midst of a famine.

3. Verse 16 (NKJV): "Go away from us, for you are much mightier than we."
   a. NIV: "…You have become too powerful for us."
   b. Deuteronomy 8:18: "Thou shalt remember the Lord thy God: for it is he that giveth thee POWER to get wealth, that he may establish his covenant which he sware unto thy fathers, as it is this day."

C. Kingdom Increase
1. Deuteronomy 7:13 (MSG): "He will love you, he will bless you, he will increase you."
2. Psalm 115:14: "The Lord shall increase you more and more, you and your children."
   a. *Shall increase you more and more* (HEB) = He will continue to add to you, over and above.
3. Leviticus 26:4: "I will give you rain in due season, and the land shall yield her increase, and the trees of the field shall yield their fruit."

DAYS OF PROSPERITY *Vol. 2*
Pastor George Pearsons

Walk by Faith and Love
Day #58

A. Genesis 26:14-17—Isaac Was Asked to Leave Gerar
   1. Verse 14: The Philistines envied Isaac because of THE BLESSING that was upon him.
      a. Men don't envy poverty.
      b. They envy someone who has more than them.
   2. Verse 15—The Philistines filled up the wells that Abraham dug.
   3. Verse 16—Abimelech asked Isaac to leave Gerar because he had become "mightier" and too powerful.
      a. *Mightier* (HEB) = Increase and become numerous
      b. MSG: "Leave. You've become far too big for us."

B. Genesis 26:18-21—The Philistines Kept Filling Isaac's Wells
   1. Isaac kept expanding in spite of the persecution.
   2. Verse 22—*Rehobeth* (HEB) = Room, streets, a broad and spacious place; an enlargement
      a. NLT/NIV: At last, the Lord has made room for us and we will be able to thrive and prosper in this land.
      b. MSG: "He named it Rehoboth (Wide-Open Spaces)."
   3. Verse 24: "The Lord appeared unto him the same night, and said, I am the God of Abraham thy father: fear not, for I am with thee, and will bless thee, and multiply thy seed for my servant Abraham's sake."

C. Walk by Faith and Love
   1. Hebrews 10:35 (AMP): "Do not, therefore, fling away your fearless confidence, for it carries a great and glorious compensation of reward."
   2. Galatians 6:9 (AMP): "Let us not lose heart and grow weary and faint in acting nobly and doing right, for in due time and at the appointed season we shall reap, if we do not loosen and relax our courage and faint."
   3. Proverbs 20:3: "It is an honour for a man to cease from strife."

EAGLE MOUNTAIN
International Church

DAYS OF PROSPERITY *Vol. 2*
Pastor George Pearsons

Symbols of Kingdom Prosperity

Day #59

A. Genesis 26:26-29—Prosperity Can Be Seen
1. Verse 28 (NIV/NLT): We can clearly and plainly see that the Lord is with you.
2. Verse 28 (MSG): "We've realized that God is on your side."
3. Verse 29 (GNB): "Now it is clear that the Lord has blessed you."

B. Symbols of Kingdom Prosperity
1. Zechariah 8:13 (NLT-96): "Among the nations, Judah and Israel had become symbols of what it means to be cursed. But no longer! **Now, I will rescue you and make you both a symbol and a source of blessing.** So don't be afraid or discouraged, but instead, get on with rebuilding the temple."
2. Zechariah 9:16-17: "And the Lord their God shall save them in that day as the flock of his people: for they shall be as the stones of a crown, lifted up as an ensign upon his land. For how great is his goodness, and how great is his beauty! corn shall make the young men cheerful, and new wine the maids."
   a. *Lifted up* (HEB) = Conspicuous, sparkle
   b. *Ensign* (HEB) = To gleam from afar, to be conspicuous as a signal, a flag fluttering in the wind, a sign, a banner, a token, an emblem
   c. NKJV: "The Lord their God will save them in that day, as the flock of His people: For they shall be like the jewels of a crown, lifted up like a banner over His land."
   d. GW: "On that day the Lord their God will rescue them as the flock of his people. They will certainly sparkle in his land like jewels in a crown."
3. Psalm 67:7 (MSG): "God! Let people thank and enjoy you. Let all people thank and enjoy you. Earth, display your exuberance! You mark us with blessing, O God, our God. You mark us with blessing, O God."
4. Genesis 12:2-3 (AMP): "I will make of you a great nation, and I will bless you [with abundant increase of favors] and make your name famous and distinguished, and you will be a blessing [dispensing good to others]. …in you will all the families and kindred of the earth be blessed [and by you they will bless themselves]."
5. Deuteronomy 28:10-11 (AMP): "And all people of the earth shall see that you are called by the name [and in the presence of] the Lord, and they shall be afraid of you. And the Lord shall make you have a surplus of prosperity."

      a. MSG: "All the peoples on Earth will see you living under the Name of God and hold you in respectful awe. God will lavish you with good things: children from your womb, offspring from your animals, and crops from your land, the land that God promised your ancestors that he would give you."

6. Jeremiah 33:9 (NLT): "Then this city will bring me joy, glory, and honor before all the nations of the earth! The people of the world will see all the good I do for my people, and they will tremble with awe at the peace and prosperity I provide for them."

7. Philippians 2:15-16 (AMP): "That you may show yourselves to be blameless and guiltless, innocent and uncontaminated, children of God without blemish (faultless, unrebukable) in the midst of a crooked and wicked generation [spiritually perverted and perverse], among whom you are seen as bright lights (stars or beacons shining out clearly) in the [dark] world, holding out [to it] and offering [to all men] the Word of Life, so that in the day of Christ I may have something of which exultantly to rejoice and glory in that I did not run my race in vain or spend my labor to no purpose."

C. Genesis 26:32—Isaac's Servants Hit a Gusher!
1. They struck a massive underground river.
2. Even in a time of drought, there is always more than enough.
3. Kingdom prosperity works anytime, anywhere, under any circumstance.

EAGLE MOUNTAIN
International Church

DAYS OF PROSPERITY *Vol. 2*
Pastor George Pearsons

Five Keys to Kingdom Prosperity

Day #60

Key No. 1—Seek First the Kingdom of God
1. Isaac is an example of someone who was in the world, but was not of the world.
2. Colossians 1:13: "Who hath delivered us from the power of darkness, and hath translated us into the kingdom of his dear Son."
3. We no longer live under the dominion, rule and control of the kingdom of darkness.
4. We are now operating in a new kingdom and a new economy.
5. Matthew 6:33: "Seek ye first the kingdom of God, and his righteousness; and all these things shall be added unto you."

Key No. 2—Obey God
1. Genesis 26:2: "Go not down into Egypt; dwell in the land which I shall tell thee of."
2. Prosperity is on the other side of our obedience.
3. Isaiah 1:19: "If ye be willing and obedient, ye shall eat the good of the land."
4. NLT-96: "…You will eat the best of the land."
5. MSG: "If you'll willingly obey, you'll feast like kings."

Key No. 3—Sow Seed and Tithe
1. Genesis 26:12: "Then Isaac sowed in that land, and received in the same year an hundredfold: and the Lord blessed him."
2. It is always a good time to sow into the kingdom of God, in spite of the economic conditions.
3. We know Isaac tithed—because Abraham tithed.
4. Genesis 14:20: "[Abraham] gave him tithes of all."
5. Genesis 18:19: "For I know him, that he will command his children and his household after him, and they shall keep the way of the Lord."

Key No. 4—Walk by Faith and Love
1. Genesis 26:21—They dug another well.
2. Hebrews 10:35 (AMP): "Do not, therefore, fling away your fearless confidence, for it carries a great and glorious compensation of reward."

3. Galatians 6:9 (AMP): "Let us not lose heart and grow weary and faint in acting nobly and doing right, for in due time and at the appointed season we shall reap, if we do not loosen and relax our courage and faint."
4. Genesis 13:8: "Abram said unto Lot, Let there be no strife, I pray thee, between me and thee, and between my herdmen and thy herdmen; for we be brethren."
5. Proverbs 20:3: "It is an honour for a man to cease from strife."

Key No. 5—Be a Symbol and a Source of Kingdom Prosperity
1. Genesis 26:28: "…We saw certainly that the Lord was with thee."
2. NIV/NLT: We can clearly and plainly see that the Lord is with you.
3. Zechariah 8:13 (NLT-96): "Among the nations, Judah and Israel had become symbols of what it means to be cursed. But no longer! Now, I will rescue you and make you both a symbol and a source of blessing."
4. Genesis 12:2-3 (AMP): "I will make of you a great nation and I will bless you [with abundant increase of favors] and make your name famous and distinguished, and you will be a blessing [dispensing good to others]. …in you will all the families and kindred of the earth be blessed [and by you they will bless themselves]."
5. Psalm 67:7 (MSG): "You mark us with blessing, O God."

Word From the Lord Through Kenneth Copeland

Southwest Believers' Convention
August 4, 2009

No, no, no, no this is not the time, saith The LORD, of the downfall of your nation. Your nation is under covenant with Me, saith The LORD. You are witnessing not the failure of the United States, you are witnessing the failure of a worldly financial system that has eroded over the years. My Word of prosperity, My Word of function, My Word that this nation began on and prospered beyond any nation in the history of this world.

No, the United States is not falling, No! I will not allow that to happen, says the Spirit of Grace. How foolish do you think I am, to allow the cradle of the gospel to fall from its limb? How foolish do you think I am?

No, I remember your deeds. I remember the gospel that's come from this nation. I remember, saith The LORD, that this is the most giving nation in history, and I will not, I will not, I will not let you go.

No, no, no, no, your finest hour is yet to come, and it is on its way, and it's being born at this very time.

No, no, no, I did not bring this financial disaster on this nation. Now some have said this is judgment. It is judgment, but I'm not bringing judgment on this nation. The seed of sin and Babylonian-world thinking has in itself its own judgment and its own disaster. And when you continue to walk out of line with My Word and My plan and My way, you will eventually fail. It's not this nation that's failing, it is the system that it has eroded into by getting away from My Word and depending on Me. But fear not, I have My eye on it, and it will go only so far and no further, saith The LORD. Hallelujah. And you will see it, you will see it, you will be in it, you will be involved in the greatest spiritual awakening that this nation has ever seen. This is My time, saith God.

DAYS OF PROSPERITY *Vol. 2*
Pastor George Pearsons

A Prosperous Journey
Day #61

A. 3 John 1-2—The Priority Placed on Prosperity
1. The Apostle John was older at this point in his life.
    a. AMP: The elderly elder of the church addresses this letter.
    b. DRB: The Ancient
2. He had walked with Jesus most all of his life.
    a. He studied after and served Jesus.
    b. He called himself "the disciple whom Jesus loved" (John 21:20).
    c. He was entrusted with the care of Jesus' mother.
3. He had become a wise, mature and honored leader in the church.
    a. His leadership and integrity were unquestioned.
    b. His humility was unparalleled.
        i. Revelation 1:9: "I John, who also am your brother…."
4. Jesus appeared to him on the island of Patmos and personally revealed the end-time plan of God.
5. It would do us well to pay very close attention to what a seasoned elder is referring to when he says, "I pray above all things that you may prosper and be in health, even as your soul prospers."

B. Prosperity Defined
1. *Prosper* (GK) EUHODOS = help on the road
2. A prosperous journey
    a. A happy journey on a particular road
    b. To be on the right, profitable path that leads to real success and good fortune
3. To be successful
    a. To succeed in reaching your destination
    b. To succeed in business affairs
4. To grant a prosperous and expeditious journey
    a. To lead by a direct and easy way
5. *To prosper* is to excel and succeed at something desirable, and to advance to the highest place possible.

C. Romans 1:8-10—A Prosperous Journey

    1. Verse 10: "Making request, if by any means now at length I might have a prosperous journey by the will of God to come unto you."

    2. Joshua 1:8: "This book of the law shall not depart out of thy mouth; but thou shalt meditate therein day and night, that thou mayest observe to do according to all that is written therein: for then thou shalt make thy way prosperous, and then thou shalt have good success."

        a. *Way* (HEB) = a journey, road, way, path

    3. Proverbs 4:18: "But the path of the just is as the shining light, that shineth more and more unto the perfect day."

        a. AMP: "But the path of the [uncompromising] just and righteousness is like the light of dawn, that shines more and more (brighter and clearer) until [it reaches its full strength and glory in] the perfect day [to be prepared]."

DAYS OF PROSPERITY *Vol. 2*
Pastor George Pearsons

The Full Scope of Prosperity
Day #62

A. **3 John 2: "Beloved, I wish above all things that thou mayest prosper and be in health, even as thy soul prospereth."**
   1. *Prosperity* (GK) = help along the way; a prosperous journey
   2. To prosper is to succeed at everything we do.
      a. AMP: "Beloved, I pray that you may prosper in every way and [that your body] may keep well, even as [I know] your soul keeps well and prospers."
      b. BBE: "My loved one, it is my prayer that you may do well in all things, and be healthy in body, even as your soul does well."
      c. WNT: "My dear friend, I pray that you may in all respects prosper and enjoy good health, just as your soul already prospers."
   3. Prosperity is more than money—it encompasses the entire scope and spectrum of our lives.
   4. Ephesians 1:3: "Blessed be the God and Father of our Lord Jesus Christ, who hath blessed us with all spiritual blessings in heavenly places in Christ."
   5. 2 Peter 1:2-4: "Grace and peace be multiplied unto you through the knowledge of God, and of Jesus our Lord, according as his divine power hath give unto us all things that pertain unto life and godliness, through the knowledge of him that hath called us to glory and virtue: Whereby are given unto us exceeding great and precious promises: that by these ye might be partakers of the divine nature, having escaped the corruption that is in the world through lust."

B. **Whatever We Do Shall Prosper**
   1. Psalm 1:1-3: "Blessed is the man that walketh not in the counsel of the ungodly, nor standeth in the way of sinners, nor sitteth in the seat of the scornful. But his delight is in the law of the Lord; and in his law doth he meditate day and night. And he shall be like a tree planted by the rivers of water, that bringeth forth his fruit in his season; his leaf also shall not wither; and whatsoever he doeth shall prosper."
   2. Deuteronomy 29:9: "Keep therefore the words of this covenant, and do them, that ye may prosper in all that ye do."
   3. Genesis 39—Everything Joseph did prospered
      a. Verse 2: "The Lord was with Joseph, and he was a prosperous man...."
      b. Verse 3: "...The Lord made all that he did to prosper in his hand."

c. Verse 5: "…The blessing of the Lord was upon all that he had in the house, and in the field."

d. Verse 23: "…That which he did, the Lord made it to prosper."

4. Psalm 112—The profile of a prosperous believer

5. Joshua 1:7-8 (NKJV): "Be strong and very courageous, that you may observe to do according to all the law which Moses My servant commanded you: do not turn from it to the right hand or to the left, that you may prosper wherever you go. This Book of the Law shall not depart from your mouth, but you shall meditate in it day and night, that you may observe to do according to all that is written in it. For then you will make your way prosperous, and then you will have good success."

C. **Prosperity includes success in every realm of life—spirit, soul, body, financial, relational, political.**

1. Spiritual prosperity
   a. Born again and spirit filled
   b. Fellowship with the Father
   c. Working with the Father in prayer
   d. Effective soul winner
   e. Revelation of the Word

2. Prosperity of the soul—mind, will, emotions
   a. Peace in your mind
   b. Alignment of your will to God's will
   c. Stability in your emotions

3. Physical prosperity
   a. Living in divine health
   b. Protection
   c. Fear free

4. Financial prosperity
   a. Increase and abundance
   b. Bills paid
   c. Debt freedom
   d. Success in all endeavors

5. Relational prosperity
   a. Love in your home
   b. Devotion in marriage
   c. Obedient children
   d. Healthy relationships
   e. Friends

6. Political prosperity
   a. A God-fearing nation
   b. Godly leadership
   c. Support for Israel

EAGLE MOUNTAIN
International Church

DAYS OF PROSPERITY *Vol. 2*
Pastor George Pearsons

Prospering Beyond Human Reason

Day #63

A. It Is My Desire to Prosper You Beyond Human Reason
Word from the Lord through Kenneth Copeland
Monday, April 25, 2011, ICFM 33rd Convention

1. "Don't you remember in My WORD that it says, Eye has not seen, neither have ear heard, neither has entered into the heart of man what I have in store for those that love me? Do you remember My WORD saying that, saith The LORD?"

2. "Remember—My plan for all men for all time was the Garden of Eden. My plan was that that should have been the worst condition the human man would have ever seen because it was all good from there on."

3. "Far richer than that Garden. That was not man's best."

4. "THE BLESSING of Abraham is the Eden covenant—but you'll have to listen to Me, saith The LORD. Adam wouldn't listen to Me, and if you don't listen to Me, I can't get into your hands what I have designed for you."

5. "But it is My desire to prosper you beyond human reason. Human reasoning is based on facts. Heaven's reasoning is based on the future of God's dreams. He knows the beginning from the end. And the end is stunning!"

B. John 6:5-9—Human Reasoning Is Based on Facts

1. "When Jesus then lifted up his eyes, and saw a great company come unto him, he saith unto Philip, Whence shall we buy bread, that these may eat? And this he said to prove him: for he himself knew what he would do. Philip answered him, Two hundred pennyworth of bread is not sufficient for them, that every one of them may take a little. One of his disciples, Andrew, Simon Peter's brother, saith unto him, There is a lad here, which hath five barley loaves, and two small fishes: but what are they among so many?"

   a. Verse 7 (AMP): "Philip answered Him, Two hundred pennies' (forty dollars) worth of bread is not enough that everyone may receive even a little."

   b. Verse 7 (NIV-84): "Philip answered him, 'Eight months' wages would not buy enough bread for each one to have a bite!'"

  c. Verse 9 (NLT): "There's a young boy here with five barley loaves and two fish. But what good is that with this huge crowd?"[1]

  d. Verses 8-9 (MSG): "One of the disciples—it was Andrew, brother to Simon Peter—said, 'There's a little boy here who has five barley loaves and two fish. But that's a drop in the bucket for a crowd like this.'"

2. Human reasoning is based on what we can see, touch, taste and hear.

3. Human reasoning is based on existing conditions.

4. Human reasoning keeps us trapped within the confines of limitation.

5. Psalm 78:40-42: "How oft did they provoke him in the wilderness, and grieve him in the desert! Yea, they turned back and tempted God, and limited the Holy One of Israel. They remembered not his hand, nor the day when he delivered them from the enemy."

C. John 6:10-13—Heaven's Reasoning Is Based on the Future of God's Dreams

1. "And Jesus said, Make the men sit down. Now there was much grass in the place. So the men sat down, in number about five thousand. And Jesus took the loaves; and when he had given thanks, he distributed to the disciples, and the disciples to them that were set down; and likewise of the fishes as much as they would. When they were filled, he said unto his disciples, Gather up the fragments that remain, that nothing be lost. Therefore they gathered them together, and filled twelve baskets with the fragments of the five barley loaves, which remained over and above unto them that had eaten."

2. God wants to prosper us beyond human reason.

  a. Beyond what we can see, touch, taste and hear

  b. Beyond existing conditions

  c. Beyond economic constraints

3. Heaven's plan is for us to establish the Garden of Eden wherever we go.

4. Don't limit God by trying to figure out how to meet your own needs.

5. Ephesians 3:20 (AMP): "Now to Him Who, by (in consequence of) the [action of His] power that is at work within us, is able to [carry out His purpose and] do superabundantly, far over and above all that we [dare] ask or think [infinitely beyond our highest prayers, desires, thoughts, hopes, or dreams]."

---

[1]John 6:7 Greek: *Two hundred denarii would not be enough.* A denarius was equivalent to a laborer's full day's wage.

EAGLE MOUNTAIN
International Church

DAYS OF PROSPERITY *Vol. 2*
Pastor George Pearsons

Claim What You Need
Day #64

A. The Lord's Correction for Kenneth E. Hagin About Believing for Finances
1. He began his traveling ministry in 1949.
2. The first year was a tremendous struggle financially.
3. Adequate provision was scarce.
   a. They lived in a three-room apartment.
   b. The children were not properly clothed or fed.
   c. The car was worn-out enough to sell as junk.
   d. The finances were not manifesting.
4. The Lord corrected Brother Hagin's thinking about how to believe for finances.

B. The Three-Step Process
1. "Claim whatever you need."
2. "Say, 'Satan, take your hands off my money.'"
3. "Say, 'Go, ministering spirits, and cause the money to come.'"
4. "Before the Lord spoke to me, I would pray, fast, weep, and cry and still barely skim by."
5. After receiving this word, Brother Hagin walked over to the church where he would be conducting a service that evening.
   a. "I stood on the platform in that empty church and said, 'I claim $150 this week. Satan, take your hands off my finances. Go, ministering spirits, and cause the money to come.'"
   b. "I tested this out time and time again. And I got the money I claimed every time."

C. Joshua 18:1-3—Claim What You Need
1. *Possess* (HEB) = to take possession of, to dispossess and drive out, to claim.
2. Galatians 6:9 (AMP): "And let us not lose heart and grow weary and faint in acting nobly and doing right, for in due time and at the appointed season we shall reap, if we do not loosen and relax our courage and faint."
3. *Claim* (Merriam-Webster):
   a. To take as the rightful owner
   b. To assert in the face of possible contradiction
   c. A right to claim or demand

4. Joshua 18:3 (GNB): "How long are you going to wait before you go in and take the land?"
5. John 14:13: "Whatsoever ye shall ask in my name, that will I do, that the Father may be glorified in the Son."
   a. GK: "Whatever you demand as your Christian rights, I will see to it that it is carried out."
6. "For all of you who will take My WORD and stand on it," saith The LORD, "the Kingdom is for you, the angels are for you, and all of heaven's reserves are at your call." —Word from the Lord through Brother Copeland, October 28, 2010
   a. Use your authority and command Satan to take his hands off your money.
   b. Release the ministering spirits to go get it and bring it to you.

D. Declare This Out Loud!

"Heavenly Father, I thank You for Your Word. Your Word is true. Your Word works for me. I give it first place and final authority in my life. I claim every need met on the authority of God's Word. I claim _____ (insert the specific amount). Satan, take your hands off my finances. Go, ministering spirits, and cause the money to come. I believe it. I receive it. I possess it, claim it and take it as my rightful inheritance. Father, I thank You for it NOW in Jesus' Name!"

EAGLE MOUNTAIN
International Church

DAYS OF PROSPERITY *Vol. 2*
Pastor George Pearsons

Three Essentials for a Great Harvest

Day #65

A. Mark 4:26-29—A Farmer's Responsibility
1. Verses 26-27: "So is the kingdom of God, as if a man should cast seed into the ground; and should sleep, and rise night and day, and the seed should spring and grow up, he knoweth not how."
2. The farmer sows the seed.
3. The farmer fulfills his responsibility.
4. "Jesus compared the kingdom of God with the planting of seed and reaping the harvest. It's a simple concept. One all of us understand. Why, then, aren't all of us producing bumper crops every season? Because we are sitting around waiting for God to do all the work." —Kenneth Copeland, *From Faith to Faith,* July 9 devotion, "Keep the Weeds Out"
5. "He doesn't operate that way. He'll work *with* you, but He won't do it *all*. There are some essential things you must do by faith if you want to have a crop to reap at harvest time." —Kenneth Copeland, *From Faith to Faith,* July 9 devotion, "Keep the Weeds Out"

B. Essential No. 1—Expect Your Seed to Grow
1. "First, you must sow the seed of the Word in faith, expecting it to grow." —Kenneth Copeland, *From Faith to Faith,* July 9 devotion, "Keep the Weeds Out"
2. Live in a continual state of expectation where sowing and reaping is concerned.
3. Luke 6:38: "Give, and it shall be given unto you; good measure, pressed down, and shaken together, and running over, shall men give into your bosom. For with the same measure that ye mete withal it shall be measured to you again."
4. Galatians 6:7: "Be not deceived; God is not mocked: for whatever a man soweth, that shall he also reap."
5. "I am expecting a record-breaking harvest."
   a. Psalm 65:11 (NLT): "You crown the year with a bountiful harvest; even the hard pathways overflow with abundance."
   b. NIV: "You crown the year with your bounty, and your carts overflow with abundance."

C. Essential No. 2—Water Your Seed

1. "Water it every day with praise. Water it with the spiritual water of the Word. That Word contains life and those seed promises can't grow without it." —Kenneth Copeland, *From Faith to Faith,* July 9 devotion, "Keep the Weeds Out"
2. "My seed always produces a bumper crop."
3. "The hundredfold return is working for me all the time."
4. Galatians 6:9 (AMP): "Let us not lose heart and grow weary and faint in acting nobly and doing right, for in due time and at the appointed season we shall reap, if we do not loosen and relax our courage and faint."
5. Hebrews 10:23: "Let us hold fast the profession of our faith without wavering; (for he is faithful that promised)."
   a. Verse 35: "Cast not away therefore your confidence [in your seed and in the Word you speak over your seed in faith] which hath great recompence of reward."
   b. *Recompense of reward* (GK) = MISTHAPODOSIA
      i.   MISTHA = pay, salary, money, recompense, restitution
      ii. PODOSIA = feet or foot (podiatrist)
      iii. Money is coming on feet in your direction.

D. Essential No. 3—Keep the Weeds Out

1. "When the weeds of unforgiveness, doubt, fear, discouragement, (and all the other junk the devil tries to sow into your crop) try to enter in, get rid of them. They'll choke the Word. That's going to take some diligence on your part. No one else will do it for you. You're going to have to weed your own crop yourself. So get tough about it. When a little weed pops up, kill it! Don't hang on to it for even a moment. Pull it up by its roots. Spray it with the Word." —Kenneth Copeland, *From Faith to Faith,* July 9 devotion, "Keep the Weeds Out"
2. 2 Samuel 23:11-12: "And after him was Shammah the son of Agee the Hararite. And the Philistines were gathered together into a troop, where was a piece of ground full of lentils: and the people fled from the Philistines. But he stood in the midst of the ground, and defended it, and slew the Philistines: and the Lord wrought a great victory."
   a. NLT: "Shammah held his ground in the middle of the field and beat back the Philistines."
   b. NIV: "Shammah took his stand."
   c. BBE: He kept his place.
3. The Philistines represent everything that would cause the fruit of our seed to be destroyed, including unforgiveness, strife, fear and doubt.
   a. Whether we bear thorns or fruit is dependent on what we do in faith concerning unforgiveness, strife, fear and doubt.
4. Genesis 2:15: "And the Lord God took the man, and put him into the garden of Eden to dress it and to keep it."
   a. *Dress* (HEB) = to work it, till it, cultivate it and develop it
   b. *Keep* (HEB) = to put a hedge of thorns around it, to watch over it; to guard, protect, defend and safeguard; bodyguard and gatekeeper

5. Malachi 3:10-11: "Bring ye all the tithes into the storehouse, that there may be meat in mine house, and prove me now herewith, saith the Lord of hosts, if I will not open you the windows of heaven, and pour you out a blessing, that there shall not be room enough to receive it. And I will rebuke the devourer for your sakes, and he shall not destroy the fruits of your ground; neither shall your vine cast her fruit before the time in the field, saith the Lord of hosts."

   a. *Rebuke* (HEB) = cripple and paralyze
   b. *Devourer* (HEB) = seedeater
   c. NLT: "Your crops will be abundant, for I will guard them from insects and disease. Your grapes will not fall from the vine before they are ripe."

DAYS OF PROSPERITY *Vol. 2*
Pastor George Pearsons

Prosperity and Patience

Day #66

A. Hebrews 6:12—Faith and Patience
1. "That ye be not slothful, but followers of them who through faith and patience inherit the promises."
2. We walk by faith and believe God to meet the need.
3. What do we do when the results seem slow in coming and we are tempted to give up?
4. We put the force of patience to work.
5. Patience is the difference between "trying faith" and "doing faith."

B. James 1:2-8—Patience's Perfect Work
1. What patience is not.
    a. Knuckling under until the storm has passed over
    b. Being satisfied with whatever happens
    c. Getting beat up with a smile on your face
2. What patience is.
    a. Undergirds and sustains faith until the result is manifested
    b. The ability to act like you have it before you see it
    c. Doesn't surrender to circumstances or succumb under trial
    d. It is constant all the time.
    e. It is courage under fire.
    f. It answers every doubt and fear with the assurance of God's Word.
3. The power of patience is a working force.
    a. Faith and patience are called "The Power Twins."
    b. They will produce results every time.
    c. Patience slips under faith and keeps it moving as time is passing.
4. Faith takes whatever you need and patience keeps it.
5. James 1:4: "But let patience have her perfect work, that ye may be perfect and entire, wanting nothing."
    a. AMP: "But let endurance and steadfastness and patience have full play and do a thorough work, so that you may be [people] perfectly and fully developed [with no defects], lacking in nothing."

C. Hebrews 10:35-36—Steadfast Patience and Endurance
1. AMP: "Do not, therefore, fling away your fearless confidence, for it carries a great and glorious compensation of reward. For you have need of steadfast patience and endurance, so that you may perform and fully accomplish the will of God, and thus receive and carry away [and enjoy to the full] what is promised."
2. Patience is a fearless confidence in God's Word that produces great and glorious results in spite of contrary evidence.
    a. When Satan brings a test or trial, do not fling away your confidence in God's Word.
    b. This refusal to cast away your confidence is the power of patience at work.
    c. Do not ever underestimate the power of progress.
3. Psalm 94:12-13 (AMP): "Blessed (happy, fortunate, to be envied) is the man whom You discipline and instruct, O Lord, and teach out of Your law, that You may give him power to keep himself calm in the days of adversity, until the [inevitable] pit of corruption is dug for the wicked."
    a. Patience is the power to keep yourself calm.
    b. Patience is the stabilizing factor in the midst of a stand.
4. The power of patience is released to work for you in the face of adversity and lack when you act on what God's Word says about your situation.
    a. Philippians 4:19: "But my God shall supply all your need according to his riches in glory by Christ Jesus."
    b. "I am confidently standing on this scripture and will not move until I see the final results."
    c. That is the force of patience in action.
5. "Adversity and lack, I speak to you in Jesus' Name. God's Word says you are defeated and under my feet. God's Word is true, regardless of what I see with my natural eyes. God's Word has a great and glorious reward of provision. I am holding fast to that Word and I will not fling it away."

DAYS OF PROSPERITY *Vol. 2*
Pastor George Pearsons

Prosperity and Diligence

Day #67

A. Who Would You Choose?

You are the owner of a very prosperous, rapidly growing company. An important position has opened up that would offer someone a tremendous promotion. After interviewing members of your staff, the decision has been narrowed down to two applicants. Each has the technical skills necessary and a vast background of experience.

At the last minute, you uncover some very interesting information. You are told that, even though the first applicant has the necessary skill sets, he is constantly late, leaves early, doesn't follow through on assignments and is undependable. He is described as being "lazy."

You are informed that the second applicant possesses the same skills, yet is extremely conscientious, reliable, thorough and takes full responsibility for her assignments. She is described as being "diligent."

Who would you choose?

The answer is very simple. Anyone would choose the person described as "diligent" over the one described as "lazy." That is exactly how God's system of promotion works. God prospers and promotes those who are diligent—conscientious, reliable, industrious, thorough and responsible.

B. God Promotes and Prospers Those Who Are Diligent

    1. Genesis 41—Joseph was working when he was promoted.

        a. Verse 12: "There was there with us a young man, an Hebrew, servant to the captain of the guard; and we told him, and he interpreted to us our dreams."

        b. Verse 41: "And Pharaoh said unto Joseph, See, I have set thee over all the land of Egypt."

    2. 1 Samuel 16—David was working when he was promoted .

        a. Verse 11: "And Samuel said unto Jesse, Are here all thy children? And he said, There remaineth yet the youngest, and, behold, he keepeth the sheep."

        b. Verse 12: "And the Lord said, Arise, anoint him: for this is he."

3. Acts 6—Stephen was working when he was promoted.
   a. Verse 3: "Wherefore, brethren, look ye out among you seven men of honest report, full of the Holy Ghost and wisdom, whom we may appoint over this business."
   b. Verse 5: "And they chose Stephen, a man full of faith and of the Holy Ghost."
   c. Verse 8: "And Stephen, full of faith and power, did great wonders and miracles among the people."
4. Luke 2—Jesus was working when He was promoted.
   a. Verse 49: "I must be about my Father's business."
5. Luke 5 (GNB)—Simon, James and John were working when they got promoted.
   a. Verse 5 (GNB): "We worked hard all night long."
   b. Verse 10: "From henceforth thou shalt catch men."

C. What Proverbs Says About Diligence and Prosperity
1. Proverbs 10:4-5—Diligent People Are Hard Workers
   a. TLB: "Lazy men are soon poor; hard workers get rich. A wise youth makes hay while the sun shines, but what a shame to see a lad who sleeps away his hour of opportunity."
   b. NIV-84: "Lazy hands make a man poor, but diligent hands bring wealth. He who gathers crops in summer is a wise son, but he who sleeps during harvest is a disgraceful son."
   c. Proverbs 13:4 (TLB): "Lazy people want much but get little, while the diligent are prospering."
2. Proverbs 21:5—Diligent People Thoughtfully Plan
   a. NIV: "The plans of the diligent lead to profit as surely as haste leads to poverty."
   b. NLT: "Good planning and hard work lead to prosperity, but hasty shortcuts lead to poverty."
   c. AMP: "The thoughts of the [steadily] diligent tend only to plenteousness, but everyone who is impatient and hasty hastens only to want."
3. Proverbs 12:27—Diligent People Are Resourceful.
   a. TLB: "A lazy man won't even dress the game he gets while hunting, but the diligent man makes good use of everything he finds."
   b. NIV-84: "The lazy man does not roast his game, but the diligent man prizes his possessions."
   c. AMP: "The slothful man does not catch his game or roast it once he kills it, but the diligent man gets precious possessions."
4. Proverbs 22:29—Diligent People Serve Great Leaders
   a. TLB: "Do you know a hard-working man? He shall be successful and stand before kings!"
   b. NIV-84: "Do you see a man skilled in his work? He will serve before kings; he will not serve before obscure men."
   c. NLT: "Do you see any truly competent workers? They will serve kings rather than working for ordinary people."

5. Proverbs 12:24—Diligent People Become Great Leaders
    a. TLB: "Work hard and become a leader; be lazy and never succeed."
    b. NIV-84: "Diligent hands will rule, but laziness ends in slave labor."
    c. 1 Kings 11:28 (NLT): "Jeroboam was a very capable young man, and when Solomon saw how industrious he was, he put him in charge of the labor force from the tribes of Ephraim and Manasseh, the descendants of Joseph."

EAGLE MOUNTAIN
International Church

DAYS OF PROSPERITY *Vol. 2*
Pastor George Pearsons

The Lord Will Furnish Your Home
Day #68

A. Psalm 112:1, 3: "Praise ye the Lord. Blessed is the man that feareth the Lord, that delighteth greatly in his commandments. Wealth and riches shall be in his house: and his righteousness endureth for ever."

"I'll never forget the time Gloria discovered that scripture. We didn't have any money at the time, and the walls in our house were as bare as they could be. But she was ready to decorate. So she took that promise, 'Wealth and riches shall be in his house' and laid claim to it by faith.

"Suddenly, everywhere we went, somebody was giving us a painting or some other little treasure for our house.

"Unfortunately, most believers aren't as quick to believe God for that kind of thing as Gloria was. Some even claim God doesn't promise us New Testament believers physical prosperity— just spiritual. But the truth is, you can't separate the two. That's why Jesus says if you'll seek first the kingdom of God and His righteousness, then all these (material) things will be added to you. He knows the spiritual realm and the material realm are connected.

"Don't let anyone talk you out of God's promises of prosperity. You don't have to choose between financial and spiritual prosperity. Both belong to you. Lay claim to them by faith. As a born-again child of God, dare to reach out and receive the riches that belong to you!"

—Excerpt of *From Faith to Faith* by Kenneth and Gloria Copeland, November 13

B. Home-Furnishing Scriptures
   1. Deuteronomy 6:10-11 (AMP): "When the Lord your God brings you into the land which He swore to your fathers, to Abraham, Isaac, and Jacob, to give you, with great and goodly cities which you did not build, and houses full of all good things which you did not fill, and cisterns hewn out which you did not hew, and vineyards and olive trees which you did not plant."
   2. Psalm 112:3 (MSG): "Their houses brim with wealth and a generosity that never runs dry."
   3. Psalm 122:7 (AMP): "May peace be within your walls and prosperity within your palaces!"

4. Proverbs 15:6 (AMP): "In the house of the [uncompromisingly] righteous is great [priceless] treasure."
    a. NIV-84: "The house of the righteous contains great treasure."
5. Proverbs 24:3-4 (AMP): "Through skillful and godly Wisdom is a house (a life, a home, a family) built, and by understanding it is established [on a sound and good foundation], and by knowledge shall its chambers [of every area] be filled with all precious and pleasant riches."
    a. Verse 4 (NLT): "Through knowledge its rooms are filled with all sorts of precious riches and valuables."
    b. Verse 4 (NIV): "Through knowledge its rooms are filled with rare and beautiful treasures."

C. Confession of Home Furnishings

Father, in the Name of Jesus,

I thank You that You provide all things richly to enjoy.

That includes the furnishing of my home.

According to Your Word, I believe I receive:

   Wealth and riches in my home.

   My house brimming with wealth.

   Houses full of all good things which I did not fill.

   Peace within my walls and prosperity within my palaces.

   Great and priceless treasure.

   The chambers of every area filled with all precious and pleasant riches and rare and beautiful treasures.

In the same way You furnished the Temple,

Thank You for furnishing my home!

House Scriptures
Is 32:17-18 New
Ps 18:19 large place
    66:12

Ps 31: 18-19
1 Cor 2:7-10 =
    Prepared !
2 Sam 7:10 KJ NIV
    "place of their own"

Prov 24: 3-4, 27 Amp timing. Ps 127:1
                    v.12 fine homes NLT
Deut 6: 10-11   8: 1-10, 18 - (fountains)

~~Ps. 68:6   Luke 4:18~~   Add : to list

Ps 107: 7-9 Amp   Prov 8:21

Ps 112: 1-5

Ps 118: 5, 23   large place

Prov 9:1   12:7   15: 6 Amp

    10:22   22:4

                        Timing =
                        Prov 24:27

Is 32: 17-18 Amp

Jer 29: 4-~~7 10-14~~   28

    31 : 12-14
                                    Amp
Ps   107:29, 29-32, 35-38, 41-43

Ps   66: 12

Ps   68: 3-6, 10 19 Amp (Luke 4:18)

Amos 9: 13-15   landscape
                        Ps 78:55 T995
Acts 17:26   Ps 16:5-6 Ps 127:1

EAGLE MOUNTAIN
International Church

DAYS OF PROSPERITY *Vol. 2*
Pastor George Pearsons

The Goodness of God

Day #69

A. Psalm 31:19—The Goodness of God
1. NIV-84: "How great is your goodness, which you have stored up for those who fear you, which you bestow in the sight of men on those who take refuge in you."
2. God's goodness is His nature.
   a. He is "Jehovah the Good."
   b. Good is who He is and good is what He does.
   c. It is the foundation of our relationship with God.
3. From Gloria Copeland's book, *Blessed Beyond Measure—Experiencing the Extraordinary Goodness of God*
   a. "Often, when I think of how good-natured God is, I am reminded of my grandfather. All of his grandchildren called him Pop. Pop was a truly good, kindhearted man, and he loved to do good things for everyone, especially his grandchildren. We quickly figured out that he would say yes to almost anything we asked him to do. I never remember him saying no."
   b. "Even before I had my driver's license, he let me drive his pickup around the Arkansas countryside. I remember times he even let me take it to the movies in a nearby town."
   c. "If my grandmother had not been there to stop him, I think Pop would have given us anything we wanted."
   d. "Although it has been many years since he passed over, every time our family gets together, we talk about Pop. It makes us happy just to remember how good he was to us."
   e. The goodness of Pop is a picture of the goodness of God.
4. *Goodness* (HEB) = good in the widest sense of the word
5. The goodness of God represents:
   a. Everything He is
   b. Everything He has
   c. Everything He desires to do for us

B. Ephesians 3:20—How Great Is the Goodness of God?

1. "The goodness of God is the greatest good that man could ever think of—only greater!"
   —Aubrey Oaks
   a. Think of the greatest good that God could do in your life—and His goodness is greater still.
   b. The goodness of God is "good" to the furthest extreme.
2. Ephesians 3:20 (AMP): "Now to Him Who, by (in consequence of) the [action of His] power that is at work within us, is able to [carry out His purpose and] do superabundantly, far over and above all that we [dare] ask or think [infinitely beyond our highest prayers, desires, thoughts, hopes, or dreams]."
3. Exodus 33:18-19: "And he said, I beseech thee, show me thy glory. And he said, I will make all my goodness pass before thee, and I will proclaim the name of the Lord before thee; and will be gracious to whom I will be gracious, and will show mercy on whom I will show mercy."
4. Exodus 34:5-6: "…The Lord God, merciful and gracious, longsuffering, and abundant in goodness and truth."
5. James 1:17 (AMP): "Every good gift and every perfect (free, large, full) gift is from above; it comes down from the Father of all [that gives] light."

C. Prosperity and the Goodness of God

1. *Goodness* (HEB) = prosperity, good things, goods, property
2. Psalm 65:11: "Thou crownest the year with thy goodness; and thy paths drop fatness."
   a. Verses 11-13 (NLT): "You crown the year with a bountiful harvest; even the hard pathways overflow with abundance. The grasslands of the wilderness become a lush pasture, and the hillsides blossom with joy. The meadows are clothed with flocks of sheep, and the valleys are carpeted with grain."
   b. Verse 11 (NIV): "You crown the year with your bounty, and your carts overflow with abundance."
3. Psalm 107:8-9: "Oh that men would praise the Lord for his goodness, and for his wonderful works to the children of men! For he satisfieth the longing soul, and filleth the hungry soul with goodness."
   a. Psalm 34:8-10: "O taste and see that the Lord is good: blessed is the man that trusteth in him. O fear the Lord, ye his saints: for there is no want to them that fear him. The young lions do lack, and suffer hunger: but they that seek the Lord shall not want any good thing."
4. Psalm 16:2 (NLT): "Every good thing I have comes from you."
   a. NIV: "Apart from you I have no good thing."
   b. AMP: "I say to the Lord, You are my Lord; I have no good beside or beyond You."
5. Psalm 23:6: "Surely goodness and mercy shall follow me all the days of my life."
   a. *Follow* (HEB) = to pursue, chase after, protect from behind
   b. God's goodness is pursuing us, chasing after us and is protecting us from behind.
   c. Deuteronomy 28:2: "And all these blessings shall come on thee, and overtake thee."

DAYS OF PROSPERITY *Vol. 2*
Pastor George Pearsons

Get Back Up on Your Faith

Day #70

A. Luke 8:22-25—Where Is Your Faith?

1. Of all the things Jesus could have said to the disciples, He said, "Where is your faith?"
2. In other words, "Where is your trust in what I have already told you?"
3. Too many have gotten out of faith where believing for finances is concerned.
4. The temptation is for people to give up believing God in tough times.
    a. They cast away their confidence which has great recompense of reward (Hebrews 10:35).
    b. They stop acting on and paying attention to the Word. As a result, their faith begins to slip out as a leaking vessel (Hebrews 2:1).
    c. They become weary in well doing and are not able to reap in due season (Galatians 6:9).
5. The word from the Lord to those that have let go of their faith is, "Get back up on your faith!"
    a. The stronger your faith, the easier it is to believe God for provision.
    b. Matthew 21:21-22: "Verily I say unto you, If ye have faith, and doubt not, ye shall not only do this which is done to the fig tree, but also if ye shall say unto this mountain, Be thou removed, and be thou cast into the sea; it shall be done. And all things, whatsoever ye shall ask in prayer, believing, ye shall receive."
    c. Faith is the answer to the storm.

B. Hebrews 11:1: "Now faith is the substance of things hoped for, the evidence of things not seen."

1. AMP: "Now faith is the assurance (the confirmation, the title deed) of the things [we] hope for, being the proof of things [we] do not see and the conviction of their reality [faith perceiving as real fact what is not revealed to the senses]."
2. NLT: "Faith is the confidence that what we hope for will actually happen; it gives us assurance about things we cannot see."
3. Faith says, "It is mine now!"

C. Romans 4:17-21—Faith calls things which be not as though they were.

1. Verse 17 (AMP): "As it is written, I have made you the father of many nations. [He was appointed our father] in the sight of God in Whom he believed, Who gives life to the dead and speaks of the nonexistent things that [He has foretold and promised] as if they [already] existed."

2. Verse 18: *According to* (GK) = in hearty agreement with

3. Faith is released by words.
   a. 2 Corinthians 4:13: "We having the same spirit of faith, according as it is written, I believed, and therefore have I spoken; we also believe, and therefore speak."
   b. The essence of faith is to "believe it and say it."
   c. Mark 11:22-23: "Have faith in God. For verily I say unto you, That whosoever shall say unto this mountain, Be thou removed, and be thou cast into the sea; and shall not doubt in his heart, but shall believe that those things which he saith shall come to pass; he shall have whatsoever he saith."

4. To speak the Word of God over your life is actually to prophesy.
   a. 2 Peter 1:19: "We have also a more sure word of prophecy."
   b. You are the prophet of your own life.

5. Ezra 6:14 (AMP): "And the elders of the Jews built and they prospered through the prophesying of Haggai the prophet and Zechariah."

6. Speak the word of God and prophesy over whatever it is you need in your life.
   a. 1 John 5:4: "For whatsoever is born of God overcometh the world: and this is the victory that overcometh the world, even our faith."
   b. Get back up on your faith and lay hold of what you need with your words, and don't let go until it is yours.

EAGLE MOUNTAIN
International Church

DAYS OF PROSPERITY *Vol. 2*
Pastor George Pearsons

God's Great Storehouse—Part 1
Day #71

A. **"God's Great Storehouse"**—Word from the Lord through Kenneth Copeland, Nov. 10, 2011
   1. "I have a great storehouse. Much more has been stored up in the storehouse of riches beyond your wildest dream that I laid up for you before the foundation of the world."
   2. "Much more is stored up there than what the Church has ever called for."
   3. "I never have held back on the Church," saith The LORD and the God of plenty. "I've made it available to you. I put it in My WORD. I gave you promise and stood behind it with the blood—the precious blood of your Savior."
   4. "But there has been a backwardness in My people about laying hold of the things that I have provided for you."
   5. "But I will say this: There is a people in the land. There is a people around the world. There is a people strong and mighty growing much stronger and much mightier and more bold to lay hold and put their claim of faith on the things that I have laid up for you and it thrills Me," saith The LORD, "because it's been yours all the time."

B. **"I have a great storehouse."**
   1. Deuteronomy 28:12: "The Lord shall open unto thee his good treasure…."
      a. *Treasure* (HEB) = storehouse
      b. HEB: Treasures such as silver, gold, etc.
      c. BBE: "…His store-house in heaven."
      d. CEV: "…The storehouses of the skies."
      e. NIV: "…The storehouse of his bounty."
      f. *Stone Edition Chumash:* His storehouse of goodness
   2. Hebrews 13:20-21 (AMP): "Now may the God of peace…strengthen (complete, perfect) and make you what you ought to be and equip you with everything good that you may carry out His will."
      a. Make you perfect (GK)—to outfit
   3. Psalm 31:19 (NIV-84): "How great is your goodness, which you have stored up for those who fear you, which you bestow in the sight of men on those who take refuge in you."
      a. *Goodness* (HEB) = prosperity, good things, property

4. Proverbs 2:6-7 (NIV-84): "For the Lord gives wisdom, and from his mouth come knowledge and understanding. He holds victory [KJV: wisdom] in store for the upright, he is a shield to those whose walk is blameless."

5. 2 Peter 1:2-3 (AMP): "May grace (God's favor) and peace (which is perfect well-being, all necessary good, all spiritual prosperity, and freedom from fears and agitating passions and moral conflicts) be multiplied to you in [the full, personal, precise, and correct] knowledge of God and of Jesus our Lord. For His divine power has bestowed upon us all things that [are requisite and suited] to life and godliness, through the [full, personal] knowledge of Him Who called us by and to His own glory and excellence (virtue)."

C. **"Much more has been stored up in the storehouse of riches beyond your wildest dream that I laid up for you before the foundation of the world."**

1. Ephesians 3:20: "Now unto him that is able to do exceeding abundantly above all that we ask or think, according to the power that worketh in us."

2. AMP: "Now to Him Who, by (in consequence of) the [action of His] power that is at work within us, is able to [carry out His purpose and] do superabundantly, far over and above all that we [dare] ask or think [infinitely beyond our highest prayers, desires, thoughts, hopes, or dreams]."

3. MSG: "God can do anything, you know—far more than you could ever imagine or guess or request in your wildest dreams!"

4. Malachi 3:10 (MSG): "Bring your full tithe to the Temple treasury so there will be ample provisions in my Temple. Test me in this and see if I don't open up heaven itself to you and pour out blessings beyond your wildest dreams."

5. "I have plans that you have never dreamed of," saith The LORD. "They are beyond your wildest imagination. I did it just for you. Heaven is overloaded with things that I have prepared for your enjoyment. If you will simply come to that place where you just say, 'God, I am so grateful,' and give Me an opportunity."—Word from the Lord through Kenneth Copeland, Southwest Believers' Convention, Aug. 7, 2009

EAGLE MOUNTAIN
International Church

DAYS OF PROSPERITY *Vol. 2*
Pastor George Pearsons

God's Great Storehouse—Part 2

Day #72

A. **"God's Great Storehouse"** Word from the Lord through Kenneth Copeland, Nov. 10, 2011
   1. "I have a great storehouse. Much more has been stored up in the storehouse of riches beyond your wildest dream that I laid up for you before the foundation of the world."
   2. "Much more is stored up there than what the Church has ever called for."
   3. "I never have held back on the Church," saith The LORD and the God of plenty. "I've made it available to you. I put it in My WORD. I gave you promise and stood behind it with the blood—the precious blood of your Savior."
   4. "But there has been a backwardness in My people about laying hold of the things that I have provided for you."
   5. "But I will say this: There is a people in the land. There is a people around the world. There is a people strong and mighty growing much stronger and much mightier and more bold to lay hold and put their claim of faith on the things that I have laid up for you and it thrills Me," saith The LORD, "because it's been yours all the time."

B. **"Much more is stored up there than what the Church has ever called for."**
   1. An untapped supply exists.
      a. Unclaimed treasures of heaven are awaiting our bold claim of faith.
      b. There is supply in the storehouse that the Church has never before accessed.
   2. Isaiah 45:3 (AMP): "And I will give you the treasures of darkness and hidden riches of secret places, that you may know that it is I, the Lord, the God of Israel, Who calls you by your name."
      a. MSG: "I'll lead you to buried treasures, secret caches of valuables."
      b. NIV-84: "I will give you the treasures of darkness, riches stored in secret places."
      c. GW: "I will give you treasures from dark places and hidden stockpiles."
      d. Psalm 104:24: "O Lord, how manifold are thy works! in wisdom hast thou made them all: the earth is full of thy riches."
   3. Proverbs 8:18-21 (AMP): "Riches and honor are with me, enduring wealth and righteousness (uprightness in every area and relation, and right standing with God). My fruit is better than gold, yes, than refined gold, and my increase than choice silver. I [Wisdom] walk in the way of righteousness (moral and spiritual rectitude

in every area and relation), in the midst of the paths of justice, that I may cause those who love me to inherit [true] riches and that I may fill their treasuries."

    a. Verses 18-19 (MSG): "Wealth and Glory accompany me—also substantial Honor and a Good Name. My benefits are worth more than a big salary, even a very big salary; the returns on me exceed any imaginable bonus."

4. Psalm 103:2 (AMP): "Bless…the Lord, O my soul, and forget not [one of] all His benefits."

5. "For all of you who will take My WORD and stand on it, the Kingdom is for you, the angels are for you, all of heaven's reserves are at your call." —Word from the Lord through Brother Copeland, Oct. 28, 2010

C. "I never have held back on the Church, saith The LORD and the God of plenty. I've made it available to you. I put it in My WORD. I gave you promise and stood behind it with the blood—the precious blood of your Savior."

1. Deuteronomy 28:12: "The Lord shall open unto thee his good treasure."
    a. *Open* (HEB) = to let loose, to be thrown open
    b. MSG: "God will throw open the doors of His sky vaults."
    c. The same word *open* is used in Malachi 3:10.

2. Psalm 84:11 (AMP): "For the Lord God is a Sun and Shield; the Lord bestows [present] grace and favor and [future] glory (honor, splendor, and heavenly bliss)! No good thing will He withhold from those who walk uprightly."

3. Psalm 34:8-10 (NIV-84): "Taste and see that the Lord is good; blessed is the man who takes refuge in him. Fear the Lord, you his saints, for those who fear him lack nothing. The lions may grow weak and hungry, but those who seek the Lord lack no good thing."

4. Philippians 4:19 (AMP): "And my God will liberally supply (fill to the full) your every need according to His riches in glory in Christ Jesus."
    a. BBE: "And my God will give you all you have need of from the wealth of his glory in Christ Jesus."

5. Luke 12:32 (AMP): "Do not be seized with alarm and struck with fear, little flock, for it is your Father's good pleasure to give you the kingdom!"

6. Romans 8:32 (NIV): "He who did not spare his own Son, but gave him up for us all—how will he not also, along with him, graciously give us all things?"

7. 1 Timothy 6:17 (NIV): "Command those who are rich in this present world not to be arrogant nor to put their hope in wealth, which is so uncertain, but to put their hope in God, who richly provides us with everything for our enjoyment."

8. James 1:17: "Every good gift and every perfect gift is from above, and cometh down from the Father of lights, with whom is no variableness, neither shadow of turning.

9. Everything we need is in God's Word.
    a. 2 Peter 1:4: "Whereby are given unto us exceeding great and precious promises."

10. It is all backed by the blood of Jesus.

A Time of Great Wealth

Word From the Lord Through Kenneth Copeland
November 17, 2011

What about 2012?

It is a time of great wealth for you, a time of great opportunities. Continue to stay in My rest. Heaven's release is continuing to increase. It is building up. Enjoy it! It is working!

EAGLE MOUNTAIN
International Church

DAYS OF PROSPERITY *Vol. 2*
Pastor George Pearsons

God's Great Storehouse—Part 3

Day #73

A. **"God's Great Storehouse"** Word from the Lord through Kenneth Copeland, Nov. 10, 2011
   1. "I have a great storehouse. Much more has been stored up in the storehouse of riches beyond your wildest dream that I laid up for you before the foundation of the world."
   2. "Much more is stored up there than what the Church has ever called for."
   3. "I never have held back on the Church," saith The LORD and the God of plenty. "I've made it available to you. I put it in My WORD. I gave you promise and stood behind it with the blood—the precious blood of your Savior."
   4. "But there has been a backwardness in My people about laying hold of the things that I have provided for you."
   5. "But I will say this: There is a people in the land. There is a people around the world. There is a people strong and mighty growing much stronger and much mightier and more bold to lay hold and put their claim of faith on the things that I have laid up for you and it thrills Me," saith The LORD, "because it's been yours all the time."

B. **"But there has been a backwardness in My people about laying hold of the things that I have provided for you."**
   1. *Backwardness* (Merriam-Webster) = behind; not as advanced in learning or development
   2. Joshua 18:1-3 (NLT): "How long are you going to wait before taking possession of the remaining land the Lord, the God of your ancestors, has given to you?"
   3. MSG: "How long are you going to sit around on your hands, putting off taking possession of the land that God…has given you?"
   4. *Slack* (HEB)
      a. Postpone, put off and waste time
      b. Slow, sluggish and lazy—backwardness
      c. Easily influenced and swayed
   5. How long are you going to put off taking what is rightfully yours in God's great storehouse?

C. **"But I will say this: There is a people in the land. There is a people around the world. There is a people strong and mighty growing much stronger and much mightier and more bold to lay hold and put their claim of faith on the things that I have laid up for you and it thrills Me," saith The LORD, "because it's been yours all the time."**

1. Deuteronomy 1:8: "Behold, I have set the land before you: go in and possess the land which the Lord sware unto your fathers, Abraham, Isaac, and Jacob, to give unto them and to their seed after them."
   a. NLT: "Go in and occupy it."
   b. MSG: "Go in and take it."
2. *Possess* (HEB)
   a. To dispossess and drive out the previous tenants, expel
   b. To take possession of
   c. To claim as yours
3. *Claim* (Merriam-Webster)
   a. To take as the rightful owner
   b. To assert in the face of possible contradiction
4. Matthew 11:12: "And from the days of John the Baptist until now the kingdom of heaven suffereth violence, and the violent take it by force."
   a. AMP: "And from the days of John the Baptist until the present time, the kingdom of heaven has endured violent assault, and violent men seize it by force [as a precious prize—a share in the heavenly kingdom is sought with most ardent zeal and intense exertion]."
      i. It takes a faith-intense effort to get out of debt.
   b. NIV-84: "From the days of John the Baptist until now, the kingdom of heaven has been forcefully advancing, and forceful men lay hold of it."
   c. *Take it by force* (GK) HARPAZO
      i. Harpoon
      ii. To seize or carry off by force, catch, pluck, pull
      iii. To claim for one's self eagerly
      iv. To snatch out or away
5. John 14:13: "Whatsoever you shall ask in my name, that will I do, that the Father may be glorified in the Son."
   a. *Ask* (GK) AITEO
      i. Call for, require, demand, insist
      ii. Adamant in requiring or demanding assistance
   b. Not arrogant or rude
   c. (GK) Whatever you demand, claim, require and insist on the basis of your covenant and as your Christian right, I will personally see to it that it is carried out.
   d. It thrills God when we boldly place a demand on what is already ours and claim everything He has provided.

The Lord of the Storehouse

Word From the Lord Through Kenneth Copeland
January 23, 2012

God is The LORD of the storehouse. He is the treasurer.

Remember that lousy old saying about the king sitting in his counting house, counting out his gold? No, no, no. That's not right. Our King is not in His counting house, counting out His gold. *We* are His tabernacle. He sits on the throne of grace. He's not counting out anything. He's The LORD of the harvest. He's The LORD of the treasure. He's The LORD of the treasure house, which is part of THE BLESSING of Abraham in Deuteronomy 28:12.

That is part of what will come on us and overtake us, if we hearken to the commandment of The LORD. Jesus said, "If you do what I tell you, My Father will love you and I will love you."

Why would He hold that treasure until you got to heaven? You don't need it there. Here's where you need treasure. Here's where you need things. The treasure is on the inside of us. You activate it with the voice of faith. As you do that, it releases THE BLESSING. It goes out and causes ALL things to be added to you. It is not going to fall down from heaven. It's on the inside of you.

EAGLE MOUNTAIN
International Church

DAYS OF PROSPERITY *Vol. 2*
Pastor George Pearsons

God's Great Storehouse—Part 4

Day #74

A. **"God's Great Storehouse"** Word from the Lord through Kenneth Copeland, Nov. 10, 2011
   1. "I have a great storehouse. Much more has been stored up in the storehouse of riches beyond your wildest dream that I laid up for you before the foundation of the world."
   2. "Much more is stored up there than what the Church has ever called for."
   3. "I never have held back on the Church," saith The LORD and the God of plenty. "I've made it available to you. I put it in My WORD. I gave you promise and stood behind it with the blood—the precious blood of your Savior."
   4. "But there has been a backwardness in My people about laying hold of the things that I have provided for you."
   5. "But I will say this: There is a people in the land. There is a people around the world. There is a people strong and mighty growing much stronger and much mightier and more bold to lay hold and put their claim of faith on the things that I have laid up for you and it thrills Me," saith The LORD, "because it's been yours all the time."

B. **"But I will say this: There is a people in the land. There is a people around the world. There is a people strong and mighty growing much stronger and much mightier and more bold to lay hold and put their claim of faith on the things that I have laid up for you and it thrills Me," saith The LORD, "because it's been yours all the time."**
   1. Mark 11:22-24—We claim with our faith.
      a. Never passive, retreating, backward or shy
      b. A confident trust; fully persuaded
      c. An aggressive and forward-directed force
   2. Hebrews 10:38-39: "Now the just shall live by faith: but if any man draw back, my soul shall have no pleasure in him. But we are not of them who draw back unto perdition; but of them that believe to the saving of the soul."
   3. Mark 11:24: "…Believe that ye receive them, and ye shall have them."
      a. *Receive* (GK) = take
      b. Take with much force
      c. Seize with a grip that can't be shaken off
   4. Hebrews 11:32-34: They possessed, claimed, laid hold of and took by their faith.
      a. "And what shall I more say? for the time would fail me to tell of Gedeon, and of Barak, and of Samson, and of Jephthae; of David also, and Samuel, and of the

prophets: Who through faith subdued kingdoms, wrought righteousness, obtained promises, stopped the mouths of lions, Quenched the violence of fire, escaped the edge of the sword, out of weakness were made strong, waxed valiant in fight, turned to flight the armies of the aliens."

    b. MSG: "Through acts of faith, they toppled kingdoms, made justice work, took the promises for themselves. They were protected from lions, fires, and sword thrusts, turned disadvantage to advantage, won battles, routed alien armies."

5. We must become strong in faith in order to claim and lay hold of what already belongs to us in God's great storehouse.

    a. Caleb's faith was strong enough to possess what was already his.

    b. Numbers 13:30: "And Caleb stilled the people before Moses, and said, Let us go up at once, and possess it; for we are well able to overcome it!"

    c. Joshua 14:10-13 (NIV-84): "'Now then, just as the Lord promised, he has kept me alive for forty-five years since the time he said this to Moses, while Israel moved about in the desert. So here I am today, eighty-five years old! I am still as strong today as the day Moses sent me out; I'm just as vigorous to go out to battle now as I was then. Now give me this hill country that the Lord promised me that day. You yourself heard then that the Anakites were there and their cities were large and fortified, but, the Lord helping me, I will drive them out just as he said.' Then Joshua blessed Caleb son of Jephunneh and gave him Hebron as his inheritance."

C. Romans 4:17—We Claim With Our Words

1. Proverbs 18:20-21: "…Death and life are in the power of the tongue: and they that love it shall eat the fruit thereof."

    a. Words control the entire course of a person's future and the circumstances surrounding their lives.

    b. Words are spiritual containers that carry faith or fear, life or death.

    c. Words are spiritual magnets that draw good or bad, depending upon what is spoken.

        i. *Lasso*—a loop of rope that is designed to be thrown around a target and tightened when pulled

        ii. *Tractor beam*—a device with the ability to lock onto and pull one object to another

2. Romans 4:17: "(As it is written, I have made thee a father of many nations,) before him whom he believed, even God, who quickeneth the dead, and calleth those things which be not as though they were."

    a. NRSV: "Calls into existence the things that do not exist"

    b. GK: Calling the things not being as being

    c. "You activate it with the voice of faith. As you do that, it releases THE BLESSING. It goes out and causes ALL things to be added to you."—Word from the Lord through Kenneth Copeland, Jan. 23, 2012

3. *Call* (GK) KALEO = to summon, order and command

    a. Summons—an authoritative command demanding someone to appear in person

    b. Jury duty summons—"You are hereby notified to appear."

4. What God has provided by His grace, we must possess with our words of faith.

5. 2 Corinthians 4:13: "We having the same spirit of faith, according as it is written, I believed, and therefore have I spoken; we also believe, and therefore speak."

The Dual Nature of the Storehouse
Word From the Lord Through Kenneth Copeland
January 23, 2012

Some have thought that the storehouse was in heaven, and rightly so. Only a very few have even considered that there was a storehouse there, except to have the idea, propagated by religion, that the heavenly storehouse was to be opened only after one gets to heaven.

Nothing is any further from the truth.

Even fewer have understood the dual nature of the storehouse. Dual only in concept of the natural mind, because, you see, it is the same storehouse.

But for the sake of your understanding, the duality of the storehouse is that the storehouse in heaven is also inside your spirit man. All of it. It doesn't have to come from heaven to the earth. All things are already in the earth that you need to do the job in the earth that I called you in the earth to do. And the power that reaches out from inside you, and procures all those things, I've set aside for you, and put your name on it, [so you can] accomplish that which I have called and hold you responsible for. That power is in you and on you.

It is the power to excel. It is released by faith.

It is because of My love for you that you will come behind in nothing. No thing!

That power is called THE BLESSING. B-L-E-S-S-I-N-G that came from the BLESSED One, the BLESSED Redeemer, the BLESSED Father, the BLESSED Holy Ghost. The One who is that power has BLESSED you, and has done so in My Name and in My blood, as though you have never sinned.

So rejoice. Look to the storehouse. It is all there, and it is all waiting for My WORD to energize your faith, the key to the Kingdom, and unlock that storehouse. For as one among you recently said, this is a voice-activated system.

Activate it. Release it. And you'll surely know great reward on the earth and in heaven.

EAGLE MOUNTAIN
International Church

DAYS OF PROSPERITY *Vol. 2*
Pastor George Pearsons

The Law of Progressive Increase

Day #75

A. Psalm 115:11-14: "…The Lord shall increase you more and more, you and your children."

   1. *Shall increase you more and more* (HEB) = will continue to add, over and above

   2. "One of the most exciting things I ever discovered about God's law of sowing and reaping was the fact that financial harvests are not seasonal. If you plant year round, you can be receiving year round. If you will keep planting consistently, you will receive just as consistently. If you continually cast your bread on the water, eventually it will come in on every wave!"—Kenneth Copeland, *From Faith to Faith*

   3. There is a supernatural momentum, an exponential growth and a blessing cycle that occurs when giving and receiving are set on a consistent and uninterrupted course.

   4. That is called "The Law of Progressive Increase."

   5. The key to progressive increase is consistency.

      a. In consistency lies the power.

      b. "The longer you walk and the longer you sow and the more deposits you make, the greater your harvest will be. And soon, your tithe is what your salary was when you started. It keeps increasing and increasing and increasing. It goes from ten times to a hundred times. Do you know what I read in the scripture about God? He multiplies. He doesn't just add to us—He multiplies! Our days are multiplied. Our goods are multiplied. That is why the Word talks about abundance and abounding—these kinds of words describe God and what He does."—Gloria Copeland, *The Kingdom of God—Days of Heaven on Earth*

B. Luke 6:38—The Law of Progressive Increase: Case Study No. 1

   1. "Give, and it shall be given unto you…."

   2. Stage One: Good measure

   3. Stage Two: Pressed down

   4. Stage Three: Shaken together

   5. Stage Four: Running over

C. Mark 4:30-32—The Law of Progressive Increase: Case Study No. 2

   1. "And he said, Whereunto shall we liken the kingdom of God? or with what comparison shall we compare it? It is like a grain of mustard seed, which, when it is sown in the earth, is less than all the seeds that be in the earth: but when it is sown:"

2. Stage One: It grows up.
3. Stage Two: It becomes greater than all herbs.
4. Stage Three: It shoots out great branches.
5. Stage Four: The fowls of the air may lodge under the shadow of it.

D. Genesis 26:12-14—The Law of Progressive Increase: Case Study No. 3
1. "Then Isaac sowed in that land...."
2. Stage One: He received in the same year an hundredfold.
3. Stage Two: And the man waxed great.
4. Stage Three: He went forward.
5. Stage Four: He grew until he became very great.
   a. Verse 13 (NLT): "He became a very rich man, and his wealth continued to grow.
      i. He became the richest man in the world.
   b. *Waxed great* (HEB) = to increase, advance, be promoted, to exceed, to tower
   c. *Very great* (HEB) = speedily, quickly, rapidly
   d. HEB: "The man was great. He kept going on and was great, until he became exceeding great."
6. Stage Five: For he had possession of flocks, and possession of herds and a great store of servants.

E. The Law of Progressive Increase: Case Study No. 4
1. Kenneth and Gloria Copeland were married in 1962 and financially struggled until they heard the word of faith in 1967.
2. Stage One: They became partners with Oral Roberts for $10 per month in that same year.
3. Stage Two: They launched out in their own ministry in 1967.
4. Stage Three: They decided to sow seed and tithe and stand on Romans 13:8 (AMP) that said, "Keep out of debt and owe no man anything, except to love one another."
5. Stage Four: Over the next 45 years, Kenneth Copeland Ministries experienced "The Law of Progressive Increase." They have experienced supernatural momentum, exponential growth and a blessing cycle that is still growing because their giving and receiving has been and still is set on a consistent and uninterrupted course.

DAYS OF PROSPERITY *Vol. 2*
Pastor George Pearsons

The Laws of Poverty—Part 1
Day #76

A. Proverbs 10:15—The Laws of Poverty
1. NIV: "The wealth of the rich is their fortified city, but poverty is the ruin of the poor."
2. Poverty
   a. *Pauper* (LATIN) = a very poor person
   b. HEB: To be destitute, needy, poor, impoverished, insufficient, deficient; to live in a state of lack and extreme want
   c. The spirit of poverty has a look and an odor.
3. There are spiritual laws that govern poverty as well as prosperity.
4. There are spiritual laws that set poverty in motion.
5. "You will have to spend time in The WORD in order to get your thinking straight, your speaking straight and your actions straight. As long as you are thinking, talking and acting poverty, you are going to get more of it than you can stand—it will overtake you." —Kenneth Copeland, *Living in Prosperity*

B. Law No. 1—Don't Acknowledge God
1. "Prosperity is the result of doing God's ways."

   "Some pass the poverty test, but fail the prosperity test. You get your needs met and receive great abundance. But, your heart will begin to grow cold if you don't keep God's Word first place in your life. All of a sudden, you are taken with the things that have been added to you. They could be things like cars, planes, houses, land—whatever it is that you like. You have to walk circumspectly to walk in prosperity. You have to keep putting God first."

   "When all your needs are met, remember where you got it. Remember that it was God that gave you the power to get wealth. One thing about wealth—it can come quickly and it can go quickly." —Gloria Copeland, *The Kingdom of God—Days of Heaven on Earth*
2. Jeremiah 17:5-6 (NIV-84): "This is what the Lord says: 'Cursed is the one who trusts in man, who depends on flesh for his strength and whose heart turns away from the Lord. He will be like a bush in the wastelands; he will not see prosperity when it comes. He will dwell in the parched places of the desert, in a salt land where no one lives.'"

3. Deuteronomy 8:11, 19: "Beware that thou forget not the Lord thy God, in not keeping his commandments, and his judgments, and his statutes, which I command thee this day. And it shall be, if thou do at all forget the Lord thy God, and walk after other gods, and serve them, and worship them, I testify against you this day that ye shall surely perish."

4. 2 Chronicles 26:5 (AMP): "He (King Uzziah) set himself to seek God in the days of Zechariah, who instructed him in the things of God; and as long as he sought (inquired of, yearned for) the Lord, God made him prosper."

   a. 2 Chronicles 26:16 (NLT): "But when he had become powerful, he also became proud, which led to his downfall. He sinned against the Lord his God by entering the sanctuary of the Lord's Temple and personally burning incense on the incense altar.[2]

      i. AMP: "But when [King Uzziah] was strong, he became proud to his destruction; and he trespassed against the Lord his God, for he went into the temple of the Lord to burn incense on the altar of incense."

5. Jeremiah 17:7-8: "Blessed is the man that trusteth in the Lord, and whose hope the Lord is. For he shall be as a tree planted by the waters."

6. Proverbs 3:6 (NKJV): "In all your ways acknowledge (know) him, and He shall direct your paths."

C. Law No. 2—Don't Exercise Self-Control

1. Proverbs 21:17 (NIV-84): "He who loves pleasure will become poor; whoever loves wine and oil will never be rich."

   a. Loves pleasure more than God
   b. Loves wine and oil more than God
   c. Matthew 22:37 (NIV): "Love the Lord your God with all your heart and with all your soul and with all your mind."

2. Proverbs 23:19-21 (NIV-84): "Listen, my son, and be wise, and keep your heart on the right path: Do not join those who drink too much wine or gorge themselves on meat, for drunkards and gluttons become poor, and drowsiness clothes them in rags."

   a. Verse 21: "The drunkard and the glutton shall come to poverty."

3. Galatians 6:7-8 (NIV-84): "Do not be deceived: God cannot be mocked. A man reaps what he sows. The one who sows to please his sinful nature, from that nature will reap destruction; the one who sows to please the Spirit, from the Spirit will reap eternal life."

4. Romans 6:23: "For the wages of sin is death; but the gift of God is eternal life through Jesus Christ our Lord."

5. Proverbs 16:32: "He that is slow to anger is better than the mighty; and he that ruleth his spirit than he that taketh a city."

---

[2] 2 Chronicles 26:5 As in Syriac and Greek versions; Hebrew reads *who instructed him in divine visions.*

DAYS OF PROSPERITY *Vol. 2*
Pastor George Pearsons

The Laws of Poverty—Part 2

Day #77

A. Proverbs 10:15—The Laws of Poverty
1. NIV: "The wealth of the rich is their fortified city, but poverty is the ruin of the poor."
2. Poverty
    a. *Pauper* (LATIN) = a very poor person
    b. HEB: To be destitute, needy, poor, impoverished, insufficient, deficient; to live in a state of lack and extreme want
    c. The spirit of poverty has a look and an odor.
3. There are spiritual laws that govern poverty as well as prosperity.
4. There are spiritual laws that set poverty in motion.
5. "You will have to spend time in The WORD in order to get your thinking straight, your speaking straight and your actions straight. As long as you are thinking, talking and acting poverty, you are going to get more of it than you can stand—it will overtake you." —Kenneth Copeland, *Living in Prosperity*

B. Law No. 3—Don't Work
1. Proverbs 6:6-11 (NIV-84): "Go to the ant, you sluggard; consider its ways and be wise! It has no commander, no overseer or ruler, yet it stores its provisions in summer and gathers its food at harvest. How long will you lie there, you sluggard? When will you get up from your sleep? A little sleep, a little slumber, a little folding of the hands to rest—and poverty will come on you like a bandit and scarcity like an armed man."
    a. MSG: "You lazy fool, look at an ant. Watch it closely; let it teach you a thing or two. Nobody has to tell it what to do. All summer it stores up food; at harvest it stockpiles provisions. So how long are you going to laze around doing nothing? How long before you get out of bed? A nap here, a nap there, a day off here, a day off there, sit back, take it easy—do you know what comes next? Just this: You can look forward to a dirt-poor life, poverty your permanent houseguest!"
2. Proverbs 24:30-34 (NIV-84): "I went past the field of the sluggard, past the vineyard of the man who lacks judgment; thorns had come up everywhere, the ground was covered with weeds, and the stone wall was in ruins. I applied my heart to what I observed and learned a lesson from what I saw: A little sleep, a little slumber, a little folding of the hands to rest—and poverty will come on you like a bandit and scarcity like an armed man."

3. Proverbs 20:13 (NIV): "Do not love sleep or you will grow poor; stay awake and you will have food to spare."
   a. MSG: "Don't be too fond of sleep; you'll end up in the poorhouse. Wake up and get up; then there'll be food on the table."
   b. *Sleep* (HEB) = to be slack or languid (sluggish in character; lacking force or quickness of movement, *Merriam-Webster)*, to grow old and stale
4. Proverbs 19:15 (NIV-84): "Laziness brings on deep sleep, and the shiftless man goes hungry."
5. Proverbs 10:4-5 (NIV-84): "Lazy hands make a man poor, but diligent hands bring wealth. He who gathers crops in summer is a wise son, but he who sleeps during harvest is a disgraceful son."
6. Proverbs 20:4 (MSG): "A farmer too lazy to plant in the spring has nothing to harvest in the fall."
7. Proverbs 21:5 (NIV): "The plans of the diligent lead to profit as surely as haste leads to poverty."
   a. "The thoughts of the diligent tend only to plenteousness; but of every one that is hasty only to want."
   b. *Hasty* (Merriam-Webster) = in a hurry
8. Proverbs 13:4 (NIV-84): "The sluggard craves and gets nothing, but the desires of the diligent are fully satisfied."
9. Ecclesiastes 10:18 (NIV-84): "If a man is lazy, the rafters sag; if his hands are idle, the house leaks."

C. Law No. 4—Don't Give and Tithe
1. Proverbs 11:24-28 (NIV-84): "One man gives freely, yet gains even more; another withholds unduly, but comes to poverty. A generous man will prosper; he who refreshes others will himself be refreshed. People curse the man who hoards grain, but blessing crowns him who is willing to sell. He who seeks good finds goodwill, but evil comes to him who searches for it. Whoever trusts in his riches will fall, but the righteous will thrive like a green leaf."
   a. Verse 24 (NLT-96): "It is possible to give freely and become more wealthy, but those who are stingy will lose everything."
   b. Verse 24 (MSG): "The world of the generous gets larger and larger; the world of the stingy gets smaller and smaller."
2. Proverbs 28:22 (NIV-84): "A stingy man is eager to get rich and is unaware that poverty awaits him."
3. Joshua 7-8: Achan hid the tithe in his tent and caused Israel's defeat at the Battle of Ai.
4. 2 Corinthians 9:6 (NIV): "Remember this: Whoever sows sparingly will also reap sparingly, and whoever sows generously will also reap generously."
5. Proverbs 22:9 (NIV-84): "A generous man will himself be blessed, for he shares his food with the poor."

D. Law No. 5—Don't Obey God

1. Deuteronomy 28:15 (NIV): "However, if you do not obey the Lord your God and do not carefully follow all his commands and decrees I am giving you today, all these curses will come on you and overtake you."
   a. Poverty is a curse.
   b. Deuteronomy 28:38 (NLT): "You will plant much but harvest little, for locusts will eat your crops."
2. Isaiah 1:19-20: "If ye be willing and obedient, ye shall eat the good of the land: But if ye refuse and rebel, ye shall be devoured with the sword: for the mouth of the Lord hath spoken it."
3. Job 36:11-12 (NIV): "If they obey and serve him, they will spend the rest of their days in prosperity and their years in contentment. But if they do not listen, they will perish by the sword and die without knowledge."
   a. NLT: "If they listen and obey God, they will be blessed with prosperity throughout their lives. All their years will be pleasant. But if they refuse to listen to him, they will be killed by the sword and die from lack of understanding."
   b. HEB: They will cross the river of death.[3]
4. Genesis 26: Isaac obeyed God and reaped the hundredfold return in a time of intense famine and poverty.
5. Deuteronomy 28:1-2 (NLT): "If you fully obey the Lord your God and carefully keep all his commands that I am giving you today, the Lord your God will set you on high above all the nations of the world. You will experience all these blessings if you obey the Lord your God."
   a. "And all these blessings shall come on thee, and overtake thee."
   b. Verse 2 (NIV): "All these blessings will come on you and accompany you if you obey the Lord your God."
   c. Verse 13 (NLT): "If you listen to these commands of the Lord your God that I am giving you today, and if you carefully obey them, the Lord will make you the head and not the tail, and you will always be on top and never at the bottom."

---

[3] Job 36:12 Or *they will cross the river* [of death].

DAYS OF PROSPERITY *Vol. 2*
Pastor George Pearsons

Our Generous Father—Part 1
Day #78

A. James 1:5—Our Generous God
1. NLT: "If you need wisdom, ask *our generous God,* and he will give it to you. He will not rebuke you for asking."
2. "If any of you lack wisdom, let him ask of *God, that giveth to all men liberally,* and upbraideth not; and it shall be given him."
3. NIV-84: "If any of you lacks wisdom, he should ask *God, who gives generously to all* without finding fault, and it will be given to him."
4. AMP: "If any of you is deficient in wisdom, let him ask of *the giving God* [Who gives] to everyone liberally and ungrudgingly, without reproaching or faultfinding, and it will be given him."
5. WUEST: "The giving God who gives to all with simplicity and without reserve"
6. Verse 5 is referring to the nature of God's extreme generosity.
   a. He is not just generous with His wisdom.
   b. He is a generous, liberal giver of everything.
7. God is most generous all the time. You'll never catch Him on a bad, stingy day, because He is the same yesterday, today and tomorrow.

B. Ephesians 1:3—He Has Already Generously Supplied Everything
1. The purpose of this study is to enlarge our capacity to receive the generosity of our loving, heavenly Father.
2. The more we meditate upon His generosity, the more we are able to receive all that He has already provided.
3. So many miss out on what God wants to do when they don't comprehend His immense generosity.
   a. Many think that He is holding back on His provision.
   b. "I have never held back on the Church, saith the God of plenty. I've made it available to you. I put it in My WORD." —Word from the Lord through Kenneth Copeland, November 10, 2011
   c. We can only receive as much as we allow Him to give.
4. "Blessed be the God and Father of our Lord Jesus Christ, who hath blessed us with all spiritual blessings in heavenly places in Christ."

       a.   MSG: "How blessed is God! And what a blessing he is! He's the Father of our Master, Jesus Christ, and takes us to the high places of blessing in him."

       b.   NIV: "Praise be to the God and Father of our Lord Jesus Christ, who has blessed us in the heavenly realms with every spiritual blessing in Christ."

5. 2 Peter 1:3 (NLT): "By his divine power, God has given us everything we need for living a godly life."

C. Psalm 23:1 (AMP)—"The Lord is my Shepherd [to feed, guide, and shield me], I shall not lack."

1. "Midrash Shocher Tov elaborates on how these words, 'I shall lack nothing' describes God's boundless generosity towards the Israelites in the wilderness." —*The Tehillim*

2. "Elsewhere, we find a similar statement, 'These forty years, HASHEM your God has been with you, you have lacked nothing' (Deuteronomy 2:7)." —*The Tehillim*

3. "Rabbi Judah said in the name of Rabbi Elazar: 'Travel has three detrimental effects. It wears out clothing, it exhausts the body, and if forces one to skimp on food (due to the great financial burden of travel). None of these deprivations befell Israel, who lacked nothing in the wilderness.'" —*The Tehillim*

4. "Furthermore, it is human nature that when a person welcomes a guest, on the first day of his visit he slaughters a fat calf for him. On the second day, a sheep. On the third, a hen. On the fourth day, he serves beans, and on the fifth day even less. Not so in the wilderness, as it says 'These forty years,' which represents the entire period, from the beginning to end. On the last day of the forty years God was just as generous as on the first." —*The Tehillim*

5. "Rabbi Nechemiah said: They lacked for nothing. All they had to do was say a word and their wish was immediately fulfilled. If they so much as said, 'let the Manna taste like calf's flesh,' so it did. Or, they could give it the taste of rich oil, or fine flour, or spiced wine, or sweet cakes. The Rabbis say: 'It was not even necessary for them to speak. All they had to do was to think, and their heart's desire came to pass immediately.'" —*The Tehillim*

6. Psalm 84:11 (AMP): "For the Lord God is a Sun and Shield; the Lord bestows [present] grace and favor and [future] glory (honor, splendor, and heavenly bliss)! No good thing will He withhold from those who walk uprightly."

7. Psalm 34:9-10 (NIV-84): "Fear the Lord, you his saints, for those who fear him lack nothing. The lions may grow weak and hungry, but those who seek the Lord lack no good thing."

DAYS OF PROSPERITY *Vol. 2*
Pastor George Pearsons

Our Generous Father—Part 2

Day #79

A. James 1:5—Our Generous God
1. NLT: "If you need wisdom, ask *our generous God,* and he will give it to you. He will not rebuke you for asking."
2. "If any of you lack wisdom, let him ask of God, that giveth to all men liberally, and upbraideth not; and it shall be given him."
3. NIV-84: "If any of you lacks wisdom, he should ask *God, who gives generously to all* without finding fault, and it will be given to him."
4. AMP: "If any of you is deficient in wisdom, let him ask of *the giving God* [Who gives] to everyone liberally and ungrudgingly, without reproaching or faultfinding, and it will be given him."
5. Verse 5 is referring to the nature of God's extreme generosity.
   a. He is not just generous with His wisdom.
   b. He is a generous, liberal giver of everything.

B. God's Overwhelming Generosity
1. Deuteronomy 28:2: "And all these blessings shall come on thee, and overtake thee, if thou shalt hearken unto the voice of the Lord thy God."
2. Psalm 31:19 (AMP): "Oh, how great is Your goodness, which You have laid up for those who fear, revere, and worship You, goodness which You have wrought for those who trust and take refuge in You before the sons of men!"
   a. *Goodness* (HEB) = prosperity, abundance, property
3. Psalm 35:27: "Let them shout for joy, and be glad, that favour my righteous cause: yea, let them say continually, Let the Lord be magnified, which hath pleasure in the prosperity of his servant."
   a. *Pleasure* (HEB) = delight, desire, is pleased to do
   b. Psalm 147:11 (NIV): "The Lord delights in those who fear him, who put their hope in his unfailing love."
4. Psalm 103:2 (AMP): "Bless (affectionately, gratefully praise) the Lord, O my soul, and forget not [one of] all His benefits."
5. Proverbs 10:22 (AMP): "The blessing of the Lord—it makes [truly] rich, and He adds no sorrow with it [neither does toiling increase it]."

6. Malachi 3:10 (AMP): "Bring all the tithes (the whole tenth of your income) into the storehouse, that there may be food in My house, and prove Me now by it, says the Lord of hosts, if I will not open the windows of heaven for you and pour you out a blessing, that there shall not be room enough to receive it."
   a. MSG: "Bring your full tithe to the Temple treasury so there will be ample provisions in my Temple. Test me in this and see if I don't open up heaven itself to you and pour out blessings beyond your wildest dreams."
7. Luke 12:32 (AMP): "Do not be seized with alarm and struck with fear, little flock, for it is your Father's good pleasure to give you the kingdom!"
8. Luke 15:31 (NIV): "'My Son,' the father said, 'you are always with me, and everything I have is yours.'"
   a. "All that I have is thine."
   b. AMP: "All that is mine is yours."
9. Romans 8:32 (NIV): "He who did not spare his own Son, but gave him up for us all—how will he not also, along with him, graciously give us all things?"
10. Philippians 4:19 (AMP): "And my God will liberally supply (fill to the full) your every need according to His riches in glory in Christ Jesus."
11. 1 Timothy 6:17 (NIV): "Command those who are rich in this present world not to be arrogant nor to put their hope in wealth, which is so uncertain, but to put their hope in God, who richly provides us with everything for our enjoyment."
12. Hebrews 11:6: "But without faith it is impossible to please him: for he that cometh to God must believe that he is, and that he is a rewarder of them that diligently seek him."
    a. *Rewarder* (GK) = one who pays off and discharges that which is due
13. James 1:17: "Every good gift and every perfect gift is from above, and cometh down from the Father of lights, with whom is no variableness, neither shadow of turning."

C. Matthew 7:7-11—How to Receive His Generous Supply
1. NIV-84: "Ask and it will be given to you; seek and you will find; knock and the door will be opened to you. For everyone who asks receives; he who seeks finds; and to him who knocks, the door will be opened. Which of you, if his son asks for bread, will give him a stone? Or if he asks for a fish, will give him a snake? If you, then, though you are evil, know how to give good gifts to your children, how much more will your Father in heaven give good gifts to those who ask him!"
2. James 1:6: "But let him ask in faith…."
3. Mark 11:24: "Therefore I say unto you, What things soever ye desire, when ye pray, believe that ye receive them, and ye shall have them."
4. 1 John 5:14-15 (NIV): "This is the confidence we have in approaching God: that if we ask anything according to his will, he hears us. And if we know that he hears us—whatever we ask—we know that we have what we asked of him."
5. 1 Chronicles 29:14 (NIV): "But who am I, and who are my people, that we should be able to give as generously as this? Everything comes from you, and we have given you only what comes from your hand."

DAYS OF PROSPERITY *Vol. 2*
Pastor George Pearsons

The Generous Life
Day #80

A. **Ephesians 5:1—Following The Father's Example**
1. AMP: "Be imitators of God [copy Him and follow His example], as well-beloved children [imitate their father]."
2. Philippians 4:19 (AMP): "And my God will liberally supply (fill to the full) your every need according to His riches in glory in Christ Jesus."
3. Jesus was noted for His generosity.
    a. John 13:27-29 (NIV-84): "As soon as Judas took the bread, Satan entered into him. 'What you are about to do, do quickly,' Jesus told him, but no one at the meal understood why Jesus said this to him. Since Judas had charge of the money, some thought Jesus was telling him to buy what was needed for the Feast, or to give something to the poor."
    b. Mark 12:43-44 (MSG): "Jesus called his disciples over and said, 'The truth is that this poor widow gave more to the collection than all the others put together. All the others gave what they'll never miss; she gave extravagantly what she couldn't afford—she gave her all.'"
        i. 1 John 3:17-18 (AMP): "But if anyone has this world's goods (resources for sustaining life) and sees his brother and fellow believer in need, yet closes his heart of compassion against him, how can the love of God live and remain in him? Little children, let us not love [merely] in theory or in speech but in deed and in truth (in practice and in sincerity)."
4. Jesus was and is not a cheapskate—and neither are we!
5. Our passion is to follow in His footsteps of generosity.
    a. Act like Him, talk like Him and walk in the same generosity as Jesus.
6. My motivation for accumulation is distribution.
7. True prosperity is the ability to use God's power to meet the needs of mankind in any realm of life.

B. The Righteous are Generous

1. Genesis 12:2 (AMP): "I will make of you a great nation, and I will bless you [with abundant increase of favors] and make your name famous and distinguished, and you will be a blessing [dispensing good to others]."

2. Psalm 37:21 (NIV): "The wicked borrow and do not repay, but the righteous give generously."

3. Psalm 37:25-26 (NIV-84): "I was young and now I am old, yet I have never seen the righteous forsaken or their children begging bread. They are always generous and lend freely; their children will be blessed."

4. Psalm 112:5 (AMP): "It is well with the man who deals generously and lends, who conducts his affairs with justice."
   a. Verse 9 (AMP): "He has distributed freely [he has given to the poor and needy]; his righteousness (uprightness and right standing with God) endures forever; his horn shall be exalted in honor."

5. Luke 12:33-34 (MSG): "Be generous. Give to the poor. Get yourselves a bank that can't go bankrupt, a bank in heaven far from bankrobbers, safe from embezzlers, a bank you can bank on. It's obvious, isn't it? The place where your treasure is, is the place you will most want to be, and end up being."

6. Proverbs 11:25 (NIV-84): "A generous man will prosper; he who refreshes others will himself be refreshed."
   a. Verses 24-25 (AMP): "There are those who [generously] scatter abroad, and yet increase more; there are those who withhold more than is fitting or what is justly due, but it results only in want. The liberal person shall be enriched, and he who waters shall himself be watered."
   b. Verses 24-25 (MSG): "The world of the generous gets larger and larger; the world of the stingy gets smaller and smaller. The one who blesses others is abundantly blessed; those who help others are helped."

7. Galatians 6:10 (KNOX): "Let us practise generosity to all, while the opportunity is ours; and above all, to those who are of one family with us in the faith."

8. 1 Timothy 6:17-19 (NIV): "Command those who are rich in this present world not to be arrogant nor to put their hope in wealth, which is so uncertain, but to put their hope in God, who richly provides us with everything for our enjoyment. Command them to do good, to be rich in good deeds, and to be generous and willing to share. In this way they will lay up treasure for themselves as a firm foundation for the coming age, so that they may take hold of the life that is truly life."

C. 2 Corinthians 9:6-14 (NIV-84)—The Result of Generosity

1. Verse 6: "Remember this: Whoever sows sparingly will also reap sparingly, and whoever sows generously will also reap generously."

2. Verse 7: "Each man should give what he has decided in his heart to give, not reluctantly or under compulsion, for God loves a cheerful giver."

3. Verse 8-9: "And God is able to make all grace abound to you, so that in all things at all times, having all that you need, you will abound in every good work. As it is written: 'He has scattered abroad his gifts to the poor; his righteousness endures forever.'"

4. Verse 10: "Now he who supplies seed to the sower and bread for food will also supply and increase your store of seed and will enlarge the harvest of your righteousness."
5. Verses 11-13: "You will be made rich in every way so that you can be generous on every occasion, and through us your generosity will result in thanksgiving to God. This service that you perform is not only supplying the needs of God's people but is also overflowing in many expressions of thanks to God. Because of the service by which you have proved yourselves, men will praise God for the obedience that accompanies your confession of the gospel of Christ, and for your generosity in sharing with them and with everyone else."

EAGLE MOUNTAIN
International Church

DAYS OF PROSPERITY *Vol. 2*
Pastor George Pearsons

Are You Prepared for Prosperity?

Day #81

A. Are You Prepared for Prosperity?

"…I am looking to and fro across the earth for those to whom I may show Myself strong and transfer My property and My influence in the earth out of the hands of the powers of darkness and into the hands of My people.

"Are you prepared?

"What would you do if I put you in charge?

"Would you follow the plan that the world already has that is full of confusion and doubt and unbelief, or would you dare rise up and say, 'Thus saith The LORD…'?"

—Word from the Lord through Kenneth Copeland, June 27, 2011

B. How Do We Prepare for This Great Transfer of Wealth?
1. God's Word reveals how to prepare for prosperity.
2. There is a sharp contrast between God's covenant people and the world concerning the handling of their wealth.
3. Their differing attitudes and character traits are clearly defined in Scripture.
4. Would we even know how to properly handle wealth when it came to us?
   a. What would we do with it?
   b. We must function on a higher level than the world.
5. "What would you do if I put you in charge?"
   a. Now is the time to prepare for that assignment.
   b. Now is the time to learn how to be rich—God's way.

C. Proverbs 10:22—The Blessing of the Lord, It Makes Rich and He Adds No Sorrow to It
1. *Rich* is not a bad word—it is a biblical word.
   a. To accumulate and grow
   b. To become wealthy
2. The key to biblical wealth is in how it is handled.
   a. Proverbs 1:32: "The prosperity of fools shall destroy them."
   b. Proverbs 28:10: "The upright shall have good things in possession."

3. "If you will learn to follow the inward witness, I will make you rich. I will guide you in all the affairs of life, financial as well as spiritual. I am not opposed to My children being rich; I am opposed to them being covetous. To be rich is to have a full supply and abundant provision." —Word from the Lord to Kenneth E. Hagin

4. True prosperity vs. the world's prosperity
    a. "The world's definition of prosperity is very limited in its scope—financial ability and power. In fact, it goes only this far by its own admission. The world itself admits that it has no power to overcome poverty, sickness, spiritual or social ills." —From *The Laws of Prosperity* by Kenneth Copeland
    b. "True Prosperity is the ability to use God's power to meet the needs of mankind in any realm of life." —From *The Laws of Prosperity* by Kenneth Copeland
    c. "God's power is the only power that covers the entire spectrum of human existence." —From *The Laws of Prosperity* by Kenneth Copeland

5. The difference is very clear.
    a. Worldly wealth is all about self.
    b. True prosperity is all about obeying God and serving others.
    c. The world's motivation for accumulation is acquisition.
    d. True prosperity's motivation for accumulation is distribution.
    e. The worldly rich use people to get things.
    f. True prosperity uses things to love people.

D. Become an Expert at Managing God's Resources

"In a world that believes the only reason for prosperity is to buy bigger cars and finer houses, a new Church is rising up. These believers are not deceived by greed. They know God's purposes for prosperity.

"These believers know God wants to bless His people so they can be a blessing. They know He gives us power to get wealth, so He may establish His covenant (Deuteronomy 8:18) and so we 'may have to give to him that needeth' (Ephesians 4:28).

"God wants us to minister to a world caught up in the cycle of greed and lack. We can't do that if we are wondering where our next meal is coming from. God knows that. That's why He has provided us 'all sufficiency in all things'—so we may have enough to 'abound to every good work' (2 Corinthians 9:8).

"Our part is to learn how to access His resources and how to use what He provides. You've heard people say about their money and their giving, 'It all belongs to God anyway.' That sounds good, but it isn't true. Your money isn't all God's, and it's not all yours. All wealth comes from God. And He is the One who has given you the power to get wealth. But He is very specific about what is His, what is yours and what you are to do with what He provides.

"The bottom line is this: You are blessed to be a blessing. You oversee both your and His resources. You oversee wealth He has provided for some very specific Kingdom purposes.

"Silver, gold and all the wealth of the earth are His. For too long the forces of Satan have controlled those resources, using them to drag men into darkness. Now it's time for the Church to learn what true wealth really is, tap in to the riches that spring from the Word instead of the world, and enjoy living as givers in spreading the gospel throughout the earth.

"The most powerful spiritual invasion force the devil has ever had to face since Jesus walked this earth will be the Church alive to God's purposes for prosperity. They have found more joy in giving than in anything money could buy. They allowed themselves to become experts in managing the resources God provides."

—From *Blessed to Be a Blessing* by Kenneth Copeland

Kenneth   December 5

What Riches Were Meant to Do

"Let him that stole steal no more: but rather let him labour, working with his hands the thing which is good, that he may have to give to him that needeth."

Ephesians 4:28

It always amazes me when I preach about prosperity and someone comes up to me and says, "I don't need much prosperity. I'm a simple person with a simple life. So I just ask God for enough to meet my needs."

They think that's humility, but it's not. It's selfishness! They don't realize it, but they're actually saying, "All I care about is meeting my own needs. I have no ambition to help meet anyone else's."

They could ask God for a million dollars, take out just enough to meet their needs, and give the rest away. But that doesn't even occur to them because when it comes to money, they've been brainwashed by a world that says if you have it, you've got to keep it.

That philosophy has hindered the ministry of Jesus Christ on the earth today. It has caused preachers to set aside their calling and get secular jobs just to survive. It's handicapped churches and stunted the growth of ministries that could have reached thousands more for the Lord.

It takes money to preach the gospel. Jesus Himself knew that, and contrary to what some people think, His ministry was not a poor one. He had so much money coming in and going out through His ministry that He had to appoint a treasurer. His name was Judas.

But Jesus didn't store up that money for Himself. He gave it to meet the needs of those around Him. He had such a reputation for giving that on the night of that last Passover when Judas left so abruptly, the disciples assumed that Jesus had sent him out to give to the poor.

Can you imagine how much and how often Jesus must have given to the poor for the disciples to make that assumption?

Jesus never built a worldly empire for Himself. But that doesn't mean He was poor. It means He was the greatest giver who ever walked the face of this earth, and it's time we started following in His footsteps.

Don't turn down the wealth God wants to give you just because you don't "need" it. Dare to accept it, then pass it along to those who do. Stop working for a living and start working for a "giving." Discover for yourself what riches were really meant to do.

Scripture Reading: Luke 12:15-31

DAYS OF PROSPERITY *Vol. 2*
Pastor George Pearsons

God's Instructions to the Rich

Day #82

A. Are You Prepared for Prosperity?

"…I am looking to and fro across the earth for those to whom I may show Myself strong and transfer My property and My influence in the earth out of the hands of the powers of darkness and into the hands of My people.

"Are you prepared?

"What would you do if I put you in charge?

"Would you follow the plan that the world already has that is full of confusion and doubt and unbelief, or would you dare rise up and say, 'Thus saith The LORD…'?"

—Word from the Lord through Kenneth Copeland, June 27, 2011

B. How Do We Prepare for This Great Transfer of Wealth?
1. God's Word reveals how to prepare for prosperity.
2. There is a sharp contrast between God's covenant people and the world concerning the handling of their wealth.
3. Their differing attitudes and character traits are clearly defined in Scripture.
4. Will we know how to properly handle wealth when it comes to us?
    a. What will we do with it?
    b. We must function on a higher level than the world.
5. "What would you do if I put you in charge?"
    a. Now is the time to prepare for that assignment.
    b. Now is the time to learn how to be rich—God's way.

C. Study the Lives of Lottery Winners

"Study the lives of lottery winners. They turn out badly because they are poor people with money." (Note the woman who won $1,000,000 in the lottery who wanted to keep her welfare payments of $200 per month.)

"They did not become wealthy people because they were still poor in their thinking and in their spirits. They had no clue what to do with all that money. They tend to take the 'quick grab' and leave half of it laying on the table. They were going to pay $250,000 every month for 25 years. Instead, they want the whole $12,000,000 right now. Why? Because they want to blow it. If they had any sense, they would take the $250,000 each month and make $20,000,000 each year with it." (Note the lottery winner who started a pool table repair franchise and lost $12,000,000.)

—From *True Prosperity* by Kenneth and Gloria Copeland

D. 1 Timothy 6:17-19—Instructions to the Rich
1. Paul did not exclude rich people from the Church.
2. Paul was a wealthy man.
   a. Acts 24:25-26 (NIV): "As Paul discoursed on righteousness, self-control and the judgment to come, Felix was afraid and said, 'That's enough for now! You may leave. When I find it convenient, I will send for you.' At the same time he was hoping that Paul would offer him a bribe, so he sent for him frequently and talked with him."
      i. No one expects a bribe from a poor man.
      ii. Verse 26: "He hoped also that money should have been given him of Paul, that he might loose him."
   b. Philemon 18 (AMP): "And if he has done you any wrong in any way or owes anything [to you], charge that to my account."
      i. NLT: "Charge it to me."
      ii. WNT: "Debit me with the amount."
   c. Philippians 4:18 (AMP): "I have everything I need and am amply supplied."
      i. "I have all, and abound: I am full…."
      ii. MSG: "I have it all—and keep getting more!"
3. Paul was not intimidated by wealthy people.
   a. "Charge them that are rich in this world."
   b. *Charge* (GK) = order them, command them, teach them
4. Paul understood the pitfalls of wealth.
   a. 1 Timothy 6:9-10 (AMP): "But those who crave to be rich fall into temptation and a snare and into many foolish (useless, godless) and hurtful desires that plunge men into ruin and destruction and miserable perishing. For the love of money is a root of all evils; it is through this craving that some have been led astray and have wandered from the faith and pierced themselves through with many acute [mental] pangs."
   b. MSG: "But if it's only money these leaders are after, they'll self-destruct in no time. Lust for money brings trouble and nothing but trouble. Going down that path, some lose their footing in the faith completely and live to regret it bitterly ever after."
   c. Matthew 19:23-24 (AMP): "And Jesus said to His disciples, Truly I say to you, it will be difficult for a rich man to get into the kingdom of heaven. Again I tell you, it is easier for a camel to go through the eye of a needle than for a rich man to go into the kingdom of heaven."
5. Paul's instructions to the rich
   a. That they not be high-minded
   b. Nor trust in uncertain riches but in the living God, who giveth us richly all things to enjoy
   c. That they do good
   d. That they be rich in good works
   e. Ready to distribute, willing to communicate

DAYS OF PROSPERITY *Vol. 2*
Pastor George Pearsons

Wealth and Humility

Day #83

Foundation Scripture: 1 Timothy 6:17-19
"Charge them that are rich in this world, that they be not highminded, nor trust in uncertain riches, but in the living God, who giveth us richly all things to enjoy; that they do good, that they be rich in good works, ready to distribute, willing to communicate; laying up in store for themselves a good foundation against the time to come, that they may lay hold on eternal life."

A. 1 Timothy 6:17—Don't Be High-Minded
1. *High-minded* (GK) = arrogant, haughty and prideful
    a. *Arrogant* (Merriam-Webster) = disposed to exaggerate one's own worth or importance by an overbearing manner
2. AMP: "Charge them not to be proud and arrogant and contemptuous of others.
3. MSG: "Tell those rich in this world's wealth to quit being so full of themselves and so obsessed with money."
4. Paul realized that one of the pitfalls of having wealth is the temptation to see one's self as being superior to others.
5. True prosperity walks in humility.
    a. The more prosperous we become, the more humble we should become.

B. Luke 16:19-31 (NIV-84)—The Rich Man and Lazarus
1. Verses 19-21: "There was a rich man who was dressed in purple and fine linen and lived in luxury every day. At his gate was laid a beggar named Lazarus, covered with sores and longing to eat what fell from the rich man's table. Even the dogs came and licked his sores."
    a. The rich man never reached out to the beggar.
    b. He most likely wanted him out of the way and was relieved when he died.
2. Verses 22-24: "The time came when the beggar died and the angels carried him to Abraham's side. The rich man also died and was buried. In hell, where he was in torment, he looked up and saw Abraham far away, with Lazarus by his side. So he called to him, 'Father Abraham, have pity on me and send Lazarus to dip the tip of his finger in water and cool my tongue, because I am in agony in this fire.'"
    a. The rich man began ordering Abraham to order Lazarus to go fetch some water.
    b. He would not even speak directly to Lazarus—it was still beneath him.

3. Verses 25-26: "But Abraham replied, 'Son, remember that in your lifetime you received your good things, while Lazarus received bad things, but now he is comforted here and you are in agony. And besides all this, between us and you a great chasm has been fixed, so that those who want to go from here to you cannot, nor can anyone cross over from there to us.'"
   a. Abraham tried to talk to the rich man about the beggar and about the great chasm.
   b. He completely ignored Abraham on both counts.
4. Verses 27-29: "He answered, 'Then I beg you, father, send Lazarus to my father's house, for I have five brothers. Let him warn them, so that they will not also come to this place of torment.' Abraham replied, 'They have Moses and the Prophets; let them listen to them.'"
   a. Again, the rich man is talking directly to Abraham to send Lazarus to his father's house.
   b. The rich man is not hearing Abraham.
5. Verses 30-31: "'No, father Abraham,' he said, 'but if someone from the dead goes to them, they will repent.' He said to him, 'If they do not listen to Moses and the Prophets, they will not be convinced even if someone rises from the dead.'"
   a. Now, the rich man is arguing with Abraham.
   b. The wealthy have a tendency to not listen, be prideful and act arrogantly toward others.

C. Humility Vs. Pride
1. Proverbs 18:23 (MSG): "The poor speak in soft supplications; the rich bark out answers."
   a. NLT: "The poor plead for mercy; the rich answer with insults."
   b. NIV-84: "A poor man pleads for mercy, but a rich man answers harshly."
2. Proverbs 28:11 (MSG): "The rich think they know it all, but the poor can see right through them."
3. Hosea 13:6 (NLT): "But when you had eaten and were satisfied, you became proud and forgot me."
4. Ezekiel 28:4-5 (NLT): "With your wisdom and understanding you have amassed great wealth—gold and silver for your treasuries. Yes, your wisdom has made you very rich, and your riches have made you very proud."
5. Revelation 3:17 (MSG): "You brag, 'I'm rich, I've got it made, I need nothing, from anyone,' oblivious that in fact you're a pitiful, blind beggar, threadbare and homeless."
6. Jeremiah 9:23-24 (NLT): "This is what the Lord says: 'Don't let the wise boast in their wisdom, or the powerful boast in their power, or the rich boast in their riches. But those who wish to boast should boast in this alone: that they truly know me and understand that I am the Lord who demonstrates unfailing love and who brings justice and righteousness to the earth, and that I delight in these things. I, the Lord, have spoken!'"
7. Proverbs 22:4 (NLT): "True humility and fear of the Lord lead to riches, honor, and long life."

EAGLE MOUNTAIN
International Church

DAYS OF PROSPERITY *Vol. 2*
Pastor George Pearsons

Who Do You Trust?

Day #84

Foundation Scripture: 1 Timothy 6:17-19
"Charge them that are rich in this world, that they be not highminded, nor trust in uncertain riches, but in the living God, who giveth us richly all things to enjoy; that they do good, that they be rich in good works, ready to distribute, willing to communicate; laying up in store for themselves a good foundation against the time to come, that they may lay hold on eternal life."

"Again, please note this scripture doesn't say to charge them that are rich in this world to get rid of everything they have, because God doesn't like people who have things. It doesn't tell us to save one old shiny suit and move off into a cabin in the hills and be humble. If you do that, you simply take yourself out of any position to bless anyone else in the rest of the world. That's the most selfish thing that a Christian could do.

"No, these verses simply said the rich shouldn't trust in their riches, but in God. That's an important point. It's something you'll have to deal with where your own mind and flesh are concerned, and the more you prosper, the more you'll have to deal with it.

"You'll have to judge yourself every day of your life on your own inner attitude and faith to make sure you're depending on God and not on what you have in the bank. But don't let that scare you. Just make a sober determination that you'll do it."

—From *Blessed to Be a Blessing* by Kenneth Copeland

A. 1 Timothy 6:17—Don't Trust in Wealth
    1. NIV: "Command those who are rich in this present world not to be arrogant nor to put their hope in wealth, which is so uncertain, but to put their hope in God, who richly provides us with everything for our enjoyment."
    2. NLT: "Teach those who are rich in this world not to be proud and not to trust in their money, which is so unreliable. Their trust should be in God, who richly gives us all we need for our enjoyment."
    3. MSG: "Tell those rich in this world's wealth to quit being so full of themselves and so obsessed with money, which is here today and gone tomorrow. Tell them to go after God, who piles on all the riches we could ever manage."

4. Paul understood that the rich were tempted to replace their trust in God with their trust in wealth.

5. His assignment was to lead the rich away from their trust in money and redirect their trust toward God.

B. Mark 10:17-27 (NIV-84)—The Rich Young Ruler

1. Verses 17-18: "As Jesus started on his way, a man ran up to him and fell on his knees before him. 'Good teacher,' he asked, 'what must I do to inherit eternal life?' 'Why do you call me good?' Jesus answered. 'No one is good–except God alone.'"

2. Verses 19-20: "'You know the commandments: "Do not murder, do not commit adultery, do not steal, do not give false testimony, do not defraud, honor your father and mother."' 'Teacher,' he declared, 'all these I have kept since I was a boy.'"

3. Verse 21: "Jesus looked at him and loved him. 'One thing you lack,' he said. 'Go, sell everything you have and give to the poor, and you will have treasure in heaven. Then come, follow me.'"
   a. He did not trust the love of God coming from Jesus.
   b. Jesus was calling him into the ministry as an apostle—and he traded his apostleship for money.
   c. Jesus was also looking for Judas' replacement.

4. Verse 22: "At this the man's face fell. He went away sad, because he had great wealth."
   a. KJV: "And he was sad at that saying, and went away grieved: for he had great possessions."
   b. AMP: "At that saying the man's countenance fell and was gloomy, and he went away grieved and sorrowing, for he was holding great possessions."
   c. He experienced acute unhappiness and depression over the thought of losing what he had amassed.
   d. He trusted in his great possessions more than he did in the Word of God.

5. Verse 23: "Jesus looked around and said to his disciples, 'How hard it is for the rich to enter the kingdom of God!'"
   a. The rich are entrenched in the world's system of finance.
   b. It is possible to cross over into the kingdom system, but it can be difficult.

6. Verses 24-25: "And the disciples were astonished at his words. But Jesus answereth again, and saith unto them, Children, how hard is it for them that trust in riches to enter into the kingdom of God! It is easier for a camel to go through the eye of a needle, than for a rich man to enter into the kingdom of God."
   a. "Jesus was telling him to sell and give to the poor. But why did He tell him that and we don't have any record of anything of Him saying that any other time? Because that was his problem. He was keeping the commandments. He was doing what was good. But he had this one problem. Jesus was trying to set him free so that he could trust in Him.

   "Trusting in riches is the danger of being caught up in the world's system. This world's system can only go so far. It is not the answer to every need.

   "Thank God I am not dependent upon the world's system!" —From *The Kingdom of God—Days of Heaven on Earth* by Gloria Copeland

7. Verses 26-27 (NIV-84): "The disciples were even more amazed, and said to each other, 'Who then can be saved?' Jesus looked at them and said, 'With man this is impossible, but not with God; all things are possible with God.'"

C. Who Do You Trust?
1. Proverbs 11:28 (NIV-84): "Whoever trusts in his riches will fall, but the righteous will thrive like a green leaf."
2. Psalm 52:7-8 (NIV): "'Here now is the man who did not make God his stronghold but trusted in his great wealth and grew strong by destroying others!' But I am like an olive tree flourishing in the house of God; I trust in God's unfailing love for ever and ever."
3. Psalm 62:10 (NIV-84): "Do not trust in extortion or take pride in stolen goods; though your riches increase, do not set your heart on them."
   a. NLT: "Don't make your living by extortion or put your hope in stealing. And if your wealth increases, don't make it the center of your life."
4. Jeremiah 17:5-6 (NIV-84): "This is what the Lord says: 'Cursed is the one who trusts in man, who depends on flesh for his strength and whose heart turns away from the Lord. He will be like a bush in the wastelands; he will not see prosperity when it comes. He will dwell in the parched places of the desert, in a salt land where no one lives.'"
5. Verses 7-8 (NIV-84): "But blessed is the man who trusts in the Lord, whose confidence is in him. He will be like a tree planted by the water that sends out its roots by the stream. It does not fear when heat comes; its leaves are always green. It has no worries in a year of drought and never fails to bear fruit."

EAGLE MOUNTAIN
International Church

DAYS OF PROSPERITY *Vol. 2*
Pastor George Pearsons

Beware, Lest You Forget God

Day #85

Foundation Scripture: 1 Timothy 6:17-19
"Charge them that are rich in this world, that they be not highminded, nor trust in uncertain riches, but in the living God, who giveth us richly all things to enjoy; that they do good, that they be rich in good works, ready to distribute, willing to communicate; laying up in store for themselves a good foundation against the time to come, that they may lay hold on eternal life."

A. 1 Timothy 6:17—Their Trust Should Be in God
1. Paul understood that the source of trust can shift once money enters the picture.
2. Once trust has shifted, the next step is to forget God.
3. Hosea 13:6 (NIV): "When I fed them, they were satisfied; when they were satisfied, they became proud; then they forgot me."
4. Once the rich forget God, it is downhill from there.
5. Isaiah 17:10-11 (NIV): "You have forgotten God your Savior; you have not remembered the Rock, your fortress. Therefore, though you set out the finest plants and plant imported vines, though on the day you set them out, you make them grow, and on the morning when you plant them, you bring them to bud, yet the harvest will be as nothing in the day of disease and incurable pain."

B. Deuteronomy 8:7-20 (MSG)—Make Sure You Don't Forget God
1. Verse 11: "Make sure you don't forget God, your God, by not keeping his commandments, his rules and regulations that I command you today."
2. Verses 12-13: "Make sure that when you eat and are satisfied, build pleasant houses and settle in, see your herds and flocks flourish and more and more money come in, watch your standard of living going up and up."
3. Verses 14-16: "Make sure you don't become so full of yourself and your things that you forget God, your God, the God who delivered you from Egyptian slavery; the God who led you through that huge and fearsome wilderness, those desolate, arid badlands crawling with fiery snakes and scorpions; the God who gave you water gushing from hard rock; the God who gave you manna to eat in the wilderness, something your ancestors had never heard of, in order to give you a taste of the hard life, to test you so that you would be prepared to live well in the days ahead of you."

4. Verses 17-18: "If you start thinking to yourselves, 'I did all this. And all by myself. I'm rich. It's all mine!'—well, think again. Remember that God, your God, gave you the strength to produce all this wealth so as to confirm the covenant that he promised to your ancestors—as it is today."

5. Verses 19-20: "If you forget, forget God, your God, and start taking up with other gods, serving and worshiping them, I'm on record right now as giving you firm warning: that will be the end of you; I mean it—destruction. You'll go to your doom—the same as the nations God is destroying before you; doom because you wouldn't obey the Voice of God, your God."

C. Keep Putting God First

"Prosperity is the result of doing God's ways.

"Some pass the poverty test, but fail the prosperity test. You get your needs met and receive great abundance. But, your heart will begin to grow cold if you don't keep God's Word first place in your life. All of a sudden, you are taken with the things that have been added to you. They could be things like cars, planes, houses, land—whatever it is that you like. You have to walk circumspectly to walk in prosperity. You have to keep putting God first.

"When all your needs are met, remember where you got it. Remember that it was God who gave you the power to get wealth. One thing about wealth—it can come quickly and it can go quickly."

—From *The Kingdom of God—Days of Heaven on Earth* by Gloria Copeland

DAYS OF PROSPERITY *Vol. 2*
Pastor George Pearsons

Who Do You Love, Seek and Obey?

Day #86

Foundation Scripture: 1 Timothy 6:17-19
"Charge them that are rich in this world, that they be not highminded, nor trust in uncertain riches, but in the living God, who giveth us richly all things to enjoy; that they do good, that they be rich in good works, ready to distribute, willing to communicate; laying up in store for themselves a good foundation against the time to come, that they may lay hold on eternal life."

A. 1 Timothy 6:9-10—Love God, Not Money
  1. "But they that will be rich fall into temptation and a snare, and into many foolish and hurtful lusts, which drown men in destruction and perdition. For the love of money is the root of all evil: which while some coveted after, they have erred from the faith, and pierced themselves through with many sorrows."
  2. Ecclesiastes 5:10-11 (NIV-84): "Whoever loves money never has money enough; whoever loves wealth is never satisfied with his income. This too is meaningless. As goods increase, so do those who consume them. And what benefit are they to the owner except to feast his eyes on them?"
  3. Proverbs 8:17-21 (NIV-84): "I love those who love me, and those who seek me find me. With me are riches and honor, enduring wealth and prosperity. My fruit is better than fine gold; what I yield surpasses choice silver. I walk in the way of righteousness, along the paths of justice, bestowing wealth on those who love me and making their treasuries full."

B. Psalm 34:10—Seek God, Not Money
  1. NIV: "The lions may grow weak and hungry, but those who seek the Lord lack no good thing."
  2. 2 Chronicles 26:5 (AMP): "He set himself to seek God in the days of Zechariah, who instructed him in the things of God; and as long as he sought (inquired of, yearned for) the Lord, God made him prosper."
     a. Verse 16 (NIV): "But after Uzziah became powerful, his pride led to his downfall. He was unfaithful to the Lord his God."
  3. 2 Chronicles 31:20-21 (NIV-84): "This is what Hezekiah did throughout Judah, doing what was good and right and faithful before the Lord his God. In everything that he

undertook in the service of God's temple and in obedience to the law and the commands, he sought his God and worked wholeheartedly. And so he prospered."

    a. 2 Chronicles 32:27-29 (NIV-84): "Hezekiah had very great riches and honor, and he made treasuries for his silver and gold and for his precious stones, spices, shields and all kinds of valuables. He also made buildings to store the harvest of grain, new wine and oil; and he made stalls for various kinds of cattle, and pens for the flocks. He built villages and acquired great numbers of flocks and herds, for God had given him very great riches."

C. Job 36:11-12—Obey God, Not Money

1. NIV: "If they obey and serve him, they will spend the rest of their days in prosperity and their years in contentment. But if they do not listen, they will perish by the sword and die without knowledge."

2. Matthew 6:24 (NIV-84): "No one can serve two masters. Either he will hate the one and love the other, or he will be devoted to the one and despise the other. You cannot serve both God and Money."

3. Deuteronomy 28:1-2 (NIV): "If you fully obey the Lord your God and carefully follow all his commands I give you today, the Lord your God will set you high above all the nations on earth. All these blessings will come upon you and accompany you if you obey the Lord your God."

EAGLE MOUNTAIN
International Church

DAYS OF PROSPERITY *Vol. 2*
Pastor George Pearsons

The Upright and the Wicked

Day #87

Foundation Scripture: 1 Timothy 6:17-19
"Charge them that are rich in this world, that they be not highminded, nor trust in uncertain riches, but in the living God, who giveth us richly all things to enjoy; that they do good, that they be rich in good works, ready to distribute, willing to communicate; laying up in store for themselves a good foundation against the time to come, that they may lay hold on eternal life."

A. 1 Timothy 6:18—Do Good With Your Money
1. Why would Paul have to point out the obvious?
   a. The rich had a reputation for using their money to do wicked things.
   b. Those wicked things lead to disaster.
2. Proverbs 1:18-19 (NIV-84): "These men lie in wait for their own blood; they waylay only themselves! Such is the end of all who go after ill-gotten gain; it takes away the lives of those who get it."
   a. Proverbs 28:16 (NIV-84): "A tyrannical ruler lacks judgment, but he who hates ill-gotten gain will enjoy a long life."
3. Proverbs 13:11 (NIV-84): "Dishonest money dwindles away, but he who gathers money little by little makes it grow."
   a. NLT: "Wealth from get-rich-quick schemes quickly disappears; wealth from hard work grows over time."
   b. AMP: "Wealth [not earned but] won in haste or unjustly or from the production of things for vain or detrimental use [such riches] will dwindle away, but he who gathers little by little will increase [his riches]."
   c. Matthew Henry Commentary: "Wealth gotten by dishonesty or vice has a secret curse, which will speedily waste it."
4. Proverbs 28:8 (NLT): "Income from charging high interest rates will end up in the pocket of someone who is kind to the poor."
   a. AMP: "He who by charging excessive interest and who by unjust efforts to get gain increases his material possession gathers it for him [to spend] who is kind and generous to the poor."
5. Proverbs 28:20 (AMP): "A faithful man shall abound with blessings, but he who makes haste to be rich [at any cost] shall not go unpunished."

B. Properly Handling Wealth

"The sages of the Jewish commentaries say that judgment is sometimes in riches.

"How could that be?

"For example, look at an entertainer or an athlete who never had money and is now making lots of money. He has more money than he knows what to do with. But because he is not born again, spirit filled and is living in a dark world, he won't be taking it to church. Where is he going to take it? He will take it to the drug dealer, to the beer joint and to immorality. He can buy all the immorality and drugs that he wants. That is why so many of these people are in trouble. Financially, they have the world on a string—but the world is all they have. Their money drives them to judgment.

"Whether money is good or bad depends on who has the money.

"When the righteous have money, they do good things with it. When the wicked have money, they do bad things with it. And those bad things lead to death—many times at an early age. You might ask, 'Why would that famous person throw his life away?' The reason is because he doesn't know what else to do with it. He is living in the kingdom of darkness.

"You can't look at the rich and wonder how they got their money. Money acquired by ill-gotten gain is not from God. You could be part of the mafia and have lots of money—but you probably won't live out your full number of days. What happens to all of the 'ill-gotten gained' money? It will go right into the hands of the just.

"Do you want to be one of those hands?

"Well, get it together and you can be!"

—From *True Prosperity* by Gloria Copeland

C. Luke 19:1-10 (NIV-84)—A Wealthy, Wicked Man Who Repented
1. Verses 1-2: "Jesus entered Jericho and was passing through. A man was there by the name of Zacchaeus; he was a chief tax collector and was wealthy."
2. Verses 3-4: "He wanted to see who Jesus was, but being a short man he could not, because of the crowd. So he ran ahead and climbed a sycamore-fig tree to see him, since Jesus was coming that way."
3. Verses 5-6: "When Jesus reached the spot, he looked up and said to him, 'Zacchaeus, come down immediately. I must stay at your house today.' So he came down at once and welcomed him gladly."
4. Verses 7-8: "All the people saw this and began to mutter, 'He has gone to be the guest of a "sinner."' But Zacchaeus stood up and said to the Lord, 'Look, Lord! Here and now I give half of my possessions to the poor, and if I have cheated anybody out of anything, I will pay back four times the amount.'"
5. Verses 9-10: "Jesus said to him, 'Today salvation has come to this house, because this man, too, is a son of Abraham. For the Son of Man came to seek and to save what was lost.'"

D. Psalm 73—The Wicked Who Prosper

DAYS OF PROSPERITY *Vol. 2*
Pastor George Pearsons

Rich in Good Works
Day #88

Foundation Scripture: 1 Timothy 6:17-19
"Charge them that are rich in this world, that they be not highminded, nor trust in uncertain riches, but in the living God, who giveth us richly all things to enjoy; that they do good, that they be rich in good works, ready to distribute, willing to communicate; laying up in store for themselves a good foundation against the time to come, that they may lay hold on eternal life."

A. Ephesians 6:5-9—The Wealth Mentality
1. Paul understood that the rich subscribed to a "master/slave" mentality.
2. They were accustomed to being the dictator while those around them were required to fulfill their every command.
    a. This did not just apply toward those who served them.
    b. The rich were treating their Christian brethren this way as well.
3. Paul had to address the conduct of the rich.
4. Ephesians 6:9 (AMP): "You masters, act on the same [principle] toward them and give up threatening and using violent and abusive words, knowing that He Who is both their Master and yours is in heaven, and that there is no respect of persons (no partiality) with Him."
5. Colossians 4:1 (MSG): "And masters, treat your servants considerately. Be fair with them. Don't forget for a minute that you, too, serve a Master—God in heaven."

B. 1 Timothy 6:18—That They Be Rich in Good Works
1. He admonished them to be "rich in good works."
    a. TCNT: "Urge upon them to show kindness, to exhibit a wealth of good actions."
    b. MSG: "Be rich in helping others."
    c. True wealth is found in helping others.
2. Your good works should be as abundant as your riches.
3. Matthew 5:16 (AMP): "Let your light so shine before men that they may see your moral excellence and your praiseworthy, noble, and good deeds and recognize and honor and praise and glorify your Father Who is in heaven."

4. 1 Peter 2:12 (NIV): "Live such good lives among the pagans that, though they accuse you of doing wrong, they may see your good deeds and glorify God on the day he visits us."
5. Acts 9:36 (NIV-84): "In Joppa there was a disciple named Tabitha (which, when translated, is Dorcas), who was always doing good and helping the poor."

C. Matthew 27:57-60 (AMP)—The Rich Man From Arimathea

1. Verse 57: "When it was evening, there came a rich man from Arimathea, named Joseph, who also was a disciple of Jesus."
   a. A rich man can also be a follower of Jesus.
   b. He stepped in to help Jesus' family, seeing that they did not own a tomb in Jerusalem.
2. Verse 58: "He went to Pilate and asked for the body of Jesus, and Pilate ordered that it be given to him."
   a. Joseph had great wealth—and great influence among the leadership of Jerusalem.
   b. He boldly went to Pilate and asked for and received the body of Jesus.
3. Verse 59: "And Joseph took the body and rolled it up in a clean linen cloth used for swathing dead bodies."
   a. This rich man lifted the body and prepared it himself for burial.
4. Verse 60a: "And laid it in his own fresh (undefiled) tomb, which he had hewn in the rock."
   a. This wealthy man built the tomb himself.
5. Verse 60b: "And he rolled a big boulder over the door of the tomb and went away."
   a. He did all of this himself, not requiring anyone to do it for him.

EAGLE MOUNTAIN
International Church

DAYS OF PROSPERITY *Vol. 2*
Pastor George Pearsons

Warning: Beware of Covetousness

Day #89

Foundation Scripture: 1 Timothy 6:17-19
"Charge them that are rich in this world, that they be not highminded, nor trust in uncertain riches, but in the living God, who giveth us richly all things to enjoy; that they do good, that they be rich in good works, ready to distribute, willing to communicate; laying up in store for themselves a good foundation against the time to come, that they may lay hold on eternal life."

A. 1 Timothy 6:9-10—While Some Coveted After
1. Paul knew that covetousness was a great temptation of the rich.
2. He also realized that covetousness motivated people who wanted to get rich.
3. *Covetousness* (HEB) = insatiable craving, greed and lust for more—especially at the expense of others
   a. Proverbs 22:16 (NIV-84): "He who oppresses the poor to increase his wealth and he who gives gifts to the rich—both come to poverty."
   b. Jeremiah 17:11 (NIV-84): "Like a partridge that hatches eggs it did not lay is the man who gains riches by unjust means. When his life is half gone, they will desert him, and in the end he will prove to be a fool."
4. *Covetousness* (GK) = a desire for things that exceeds a desire for God
   a. Matthew 6:24 (MSG): "You can't worship two gods at once. Loving one god, you'll end up hating the other. Adoration of one feeds contempt for the other. You can't worship God and Money both."
   b. Psalm 119:36: "Incline my heart unto thy testimonies, and not to covetousness."
      i. MSG: "Give me a bent for your words of wisdom, and not for piling up loot."
5. Covetousness results in disaster.
   a. 1 Timothy 6:9-10 (MSG): "But if it's only money these leaders are after, they'll self-destruct in no time. Lust for money brings trouble and nothing but trouble. Going down that path, some lose their footing in the faith completely and live to regret it bitterly ever after."
   b. Verse 9 (NLT): "But people who long to be rich fall into temptation and are trapped by many foolish and harmful desires that plunge them into ruin and destruction."

101

    c.   Proverbs 15:27 (NIV-84): "A greedy man brings trouble to his family."
        i.   NLT: "Greed brings grief to the whole family."
    d.   Ecclesiastes 5:13 (NLT): "Hoarding riches harms the saver."

B. Disastrous Results of Covetousness

1. 2 Kings 5:27—Gehazi was the shrewd servant of Elisha. Even though Elisha refused payment for the healing of Naaman, Gehazi's greed got the best of him. He collected payment anyway and ended up with leprosy as punishment.
2. 2 Chronicles 26:5, 16, 21—As long as King Uzziah sought the Lord, God made him to prosper. But the stronger he got, the more greedy and prideful he became. The result was destruction. He became a leper and remained so until his death.
3. Matthew 26:14-16, 27:3-5—Judas hung himself for betraying Jesus for thirty pieces of silver.
4. Acts 5:1-11—Ananias and Sapphira fell dead for holding back their money and lying about it.
5. Take note of present-day examples of covetousness—those involved in "Ponzi schemes."

C. Luke 12:13-21—Warning: Beware of Covetousness

1. Verse 13: "And one of the company said unto him, Master, speak to my brother, that he divide the inheritance with me."
2. Verse 14: "And he said unto him, Man, who made me a judge or a divider over you?"
3. Verse 15: "And he said unto them, Take heed, and beware of covetousness: for a man's life consisteth not in the abundance of the things which he possesseth."
4. Verses 16-17: "And he spake a parable unto them, saying, The ground of a certain rich man brought forth plentifully: And he thought within himself, saying, What shall I do, because I have no room where to bestow my fruits?"
5. Verse 18: "And he said, This will I do: I will pull down my barns, and build greater; and there will I bestow all my fruits and my goods."
6. Verse 19: "And I will say to my soul, Soul, thou hast much goods laid up for many years; take thine ease, eat, drink, and be merry."
7. Verse 20: "But God said unto him, Thou fool, this night thy soul shall be required of thee: then whose shall those things be, which thou hast provided?"
8. Verse 21: "So is he that layeth up treasure for himself, and is not rich toward God."

DAYS OF PROSPERITY *Vol. 2*
Pastor George Pearsons

The Profile of a Wealthy Believer

Day #90

Foundation Scripture: 1 Timothy 6:17-19
"Charge them that are rich in this world, that they be not highminded, nor trust in uncertain riches, but in the living God, who giveth us richly all things to enjoy; that they do good, that they be rich in good works, ready to distribute, willing to communicate; laying up in store for themselves a good foundation against the time to come, that they may lay hold on eternal life."

A. 1 Timothy 6:17-19—Be Ready and Willing to Give
1. Paul knew that the rich had a tendency toward being tightfisted with their money.
2. He had to instruct them to be ready and willing to give.
   a. Give to God with their tithe.
   b. Give to the ministry with their offering.
   c. Give to others with their harvest.
      i. Ephesians 4:28: "Let him that stole steal no more: but rather let him labour, working with his hands the thing which is good, that he may have to give to him that needeth."
3. *Ready to distribute* (GK) = liberal in giving; generous
   a. MSG: "Be extravagantly generous."
   b. AMP: "Be liberal and generous of heart."
4. *Willing to communicate* (GK) = an eagerness to share with others
   a. WNT: Openhanded
   b. Given freely and cheerfully
5. 2 Corinthians 9:7 (AMP): "Let each one [give] as he has made up his own mind and purposed in his heart, not reluctantly or sorrowfully or under compulsion, for God loves (He takes pleasure in, prizes above other things, and is unwilling to abandon or to do without) a cheerful (joyous, "prompt to do it") giver [whose heart is in his giving]."

B. Psalm 112—The Profile of a Wealthy Believer
1. Verse 1—He is blessed because he honors God and His Word.
   a. To be blessed is to be empowered to prosper.
   b. To be blessed is also to be a blessing.

c. Genesis 12:2 (AMP): "And I will make of you a great nation, and I will bless you [with abundant increase of favors] and make your name famous and distinguished, and you will be a blessing [dispensing good to others]."

d. Zechariah 8:13 (NLT): "Among the other nations, Judah and Israel became symbols of a cursed nation. But no longer! Now I will rescue you and make you both a symbol and a source of blessing."

2. Verse 2—His children are blessed because of his giving.

a. NLT: "Their children will be successful everywhere; an entire generation of godly people will be blessed."

b. Psalm 25:12-13 (NIV-84): "Who, then, is the man that fears the Lord? He will instruct him in the way chosen for him. He will spend his days in prosperity, and his descendants will inherit the land."

c. Psalm 37:25 (NIV-84): "I was young and now I am old, yet I have never seen the righteous forsaken or their children begging bread. They are always generous and lend freely; their children will be blessed."

d. Psalm 128:1-3 (NIV-84): "Blessed are all who fear the Lord, who walk in his ways. You will eat the fruit of your labor; blessings and prosperity will be yours. Your wife will be like a fruitful vine within your house; your sons will be like olive shoots around your table."

3. Verse 3—Wealth and riches are in his house.

a. NLT: "They themselves will be wealthy, and their good deeds will last forever."

b. MSG: "Their houses brim with wealth and a generosity that never runs dry."

4. Verse 4—He is gracious and full of compassion.

a. *Compassion* (HEB) = a moving, a deep inner yearning, an overwhelming desire of the heart towards supplying the needs of others

b. Compassion is God's love surging through the heart of one to another.

c. Luke 10:33-35: "But a certain Samaritan, as he journeyed, came where he was: and when he saw him, he had compassion on him, and went to him, and bound up his wounds, pouring in oil and wine, and set him on his own beast, and brought him to an inn, and took care of him. And on the morrow when he departed, he took out two pence, and gave them to the host, and said unto him, Take care of him; and whatsoever thou spendest more, when I come again, I will repay thee."

5. Verse 5—He displays favor and lends.

a. MSG: "The good person is generous and lends lavishly."

b. NIV-84: "Good will come to him who is generous and lends freely, who conducts his affairs with justice."

c. Proverbs 11:24-25 (NIV-84): "One man gives freely, yet gains even more; another withholds unduly, but comes to poverty. A generous man will prosper; he who refreshes others will himself be refreshed."

d. Philemon 1:18-19: "If he hath wronged thee, or oweth thee ought, put that on mine account; I Paul have written it with mine own hand, I will repay it: albeit I do not say to thee how thou owest unto me even thine own self besides."

6. Verses 6-8—His heart is established and is not moved during adverse economic times.

a. Jeremiah 17:7-8 (AMP): "[Most] blessed is the man who believes in, trusts in, and relies on the Lord, and whose hope and confidence the Lord is. For he shall be like a tree planted by the waters that spreads out its roots by the river; and it shall not

see and fear when heat comes; but its leaf shall be green. It shall not be anxious and full of care in the year of drought, nor shall it cease yielding fruit."
- b. Psalm 1:3 (NIV-84): "He is like a tree planted by streams of water, which yields its fruit in season and whose leaf does not wither. Whatever he does prospers."
7. Verse 9—He is a giver who reaches out to the poor and continues to be promoted.
   - a. AMP: "He has distributed freely [he has given to the poor and needy]."
     - i. Our motivation for accumulation is distribution.
   - b. MSG: "They lavish gifts on the poor—a generosity that goes on, and on, and on. An honored life! A beautiful life!"
   - c. Proverbs 19:17: "He that hath pity upon the poor lendeth unto the Lord; and that which he hath given will he pay him again."
   - d. Proverbs 22:9 (NIV-84): "A generous man will himself be blessed, for he shares his food with the poor."
   - e. Proverbs 31:20 (NIV): "She opens her arms to the poor and extends her hands to the needy."
8. Verse 10—He resists the devil—and the devil flees!
   - a. Lack of any kind has no place in the house of the righteous.
   - b. The prosperous believer stands strong and firm.

C. 1 Timothy 6:19—A Foundation for the Future
1. By following these instructions, the rich will be laying up in store for themselves a good foundation against the time to come, that they may lay hold on eternal life.
2. *Laying up in store* (GK)
   - a. To treasure away
   - b. To store up a treasury
   - c. To deposit in abundance for future use
3. *A good foundation* (GK)
   - a. Something put down
   - b. The foundation of a building, wall or a city
   - c. The beginnings, the first principals, system of truth
4. That they may lay hold on eternal life
   - a. Not just for heaven
   - b. Eternal life is also the quality of life here and now.
5. Matthew 6:20-21 (NIV-84): "But store up for yourselves treasures in heaven, where moth and rust do not destroy, and where thieves do not break in and steal. For where your treasure is, there your heart will be also."

D. Are You Prepared for Prosperity?
"…I am looking to and fro across the earth for those to whom I may show Myself strong and transfer My property and My influence in the earth out of the hands of the powers of darkness and into the hands of My people.

"Are you prepared?

"What would you do if I put you in charge?

"Would you follow the plan that the world already has that is full of confusion and doubt and unbelief, or would you dare rise up and say, 'Thus saith The LORD…'?"

—Word from the Lord through Kenneth Copeland, June 27, 2011

DAYS OF PROSPERITY *Vol. 2*
Pastor George Pearsons

Supernatural Wealth Transfer

Day #91

A. Psalm 103:1-2—All of God's Covenant Blessings
 1. AMP: "Forget not one of all His benefits."
 2. MSG: "Don't forget a single blessing."
 3. "For all of you who will take My WORD and stand on it, saith The LORD—the Kingdom is for you, the angels are for you, all of heaven's reserves are at your call." —Word from the Lord through Brother Copeland, October 28, 2010
 4. God wants us to take advantage of every provisional benefit.
 5. One of those benefits is supernatural wealth transfer.

B. The Largest, Most Significant Wealth Transfer
 Word from the Lord through Brother Copeland, Branson Victory Campaign, March 8, 2012
 1. "The largest, most significant transfer of property, goods, wealth and people from the hands of the devil into the hands of God's people who are prepared to receive it.
 2. "I am telling you, the biggest transfer of property in the history of mankind has just begun and it is swinging into....
 3. "It has moved over into its final stage, saith The LORD.
 4. "And those who will listen to Me and follow Me and trust Me—those who I have taught My WORD and have given the authority to walk in these things, it is the most outstanding thing that human eyes have ever seen.
 5. "And the time is now. Your time has come. Your hour has come. So rise and do those things by faith that you know to do and all that belongs to heaven will come into your hands for your joy."

C. Financial Inversion Shall Increase in These Days
 Word from the Lord through Charles Capps, February 1, 1978

"Financial inversion [*inverted*—turned upside down, reversal in position] shall increase in these days. For you see, it is My desire to move in the realm of your financial prosperity. But release Me, saith the Lord, release Me that I may come on your behalf and move on your behalf.

"For yes, yes, yes, there shall be in this hour financial distress here and there. The economy shall go up and it will go down; but those who learn to walk in the Word, they shall see the prosperity of the Word come forth in this hour in a way that has not been seen by men in days past.

"Yes, there's coming a financial inversion in the world's system. It's been held in reservoirs of wicked men for days on end. But the end is nigh. Those reservoirs shall be tapped and shall be drained into the gospel of Jesus Christ. It shall be done, saith the Lord. It shall be done in the time allotted and so shall it be that the word of the Lord shall come to pass that the wealth of the sinner is laid up for the just.

"Predominantly in two ways shall it be done in this hour. Those who have hoarded up and stored because of the inspiration of the evil one and held the money from the gospel shall be converted and drawn into the Kingdom. But many, many will not. They'll not heed the voice of the Word of God. They'll turn aside to this and they'll turn to that and they'll walk in their own ways, but their ways will not work in this hour. It'll dwindle and it'll slip away as though it were in bags with holes in them. It'll go here and it'll go there and they'll wonder why it's not working now. 'It worked in days past,' they'll say.

"But it shall be, saith the Lord, that the word of the Lord shall rise within men—men of God of low esteem in the financial world—that shall claim the Word of God to be their very own and walk in the light of it as it has been set forth in the Word and give. They'll begin to give small at first because that's all they have, but then it will increase, and through the hundredfold return, so shall it be that the reservoirs that have held the riches in days past, so shall it return to the hands of the giver. Because of the hundredfold return shall the reservoirs be lost from the wicked and turned to the gospel. For it shall be, it shall be in this hour that you will see things that you've never dreamed come to pass. Oh, it'll be strong at first in ways, then it will grow greater and greater until men will be astounded and the world will stand in awe because the ways of men have failed and the ways of God shall come forth.

"As men walk in My Word, so shall they walk in the ways of the Lord. Oh yes, there will be some who say, 'Yes, but God's ways are higher, surely higher than our ways, and we can't walk in those.' It's true that the ways of God are higher. They are higher than your ways as the heavens are above the earth, but I'll teach you to walk in My ways. I never did say you couldn't walk in My ways. Now learn to walk in it. Learn to give. So shall the inversion of the financial system revert and so shall it be that the gospel of the kingdom shall be preached to all the world, and there shall be no lack in the kingdom. Those who give shall walk in the ways of the supernatural! They shall be known abroad. My Word shall spread and the knowledge of the Lord shall fill all the earth in the day and the hour in which ye stand. Ye shall see it and know it, for it is of Me, and it shall come to pass, saith the Lord."

"Heaven's release is continuing to increase."
—Word from the Lord through Brother Copeland, December 31, 2011

"The world says doom, and we say bloom!"
—Gloria Copeland

EAGLE MOUNTAIN
International Church

DAYS OF PROSPERITY *Vol. 2*
Pastor George Pearsons

Walking in the Word
Day #92

A. Financial Inversion Shall Increase in These Days
Word from the Lord through Charles Capps, February 1, 1978
1. "Financial inversion shall increase in these days.
2. "For you see, it is My desire to move in the realm of your financial prosperity.
3. "But release Me, saith the Lord, release Me that I may come on your behalf and move on your behalf.
4. "For yes, yes, yes, there shall be in this hour financial distress here and there. The economy shall go up and it will go down.
5. "But those who learn to walk in the Word, they shall see the prosperity of the Word come forth in this hour in a way that has not been seen by men in days past."

B. Proverbs 4:7-8—Give God's Word First Place
1. AMP: "The beginning of Wisdom is: get Wisdom (skillful and godly Wisdom)! [For skillful and godly Wisdom is the principal thing.] And with all you have gotten, get understanding (discernment, comprehension, and interpretation). Prize Wisdom highly and exalt her, and she will exalt and promote you; she will bring you to honor when you embrace her."
    a. *Principal*—first in importance, the main thing
    b. God's Word is His wisdom.
2. "God's Word is His wisdom. Giving the Word first place in your life is the only way that His wisdom can obtain its rightful position. The Bible is God's wisdom written for man. He has sent His Word to you so you can operate in His wisdom on the earth. Put the Word first in your life and exalt it, and it will exalt and promote you." —From *God's Will for You—Expanded Legacy Edition* by Gloria Copeland
3. Proverbs 4:20-22 (AMP): "My son, attend to my words; consent and submit to my sayings. Let them not depart from your sight; keep them in the center of your heart. For they are life to those who find them, healing *and* health to all their flesh."
4. You give the Word first place in your life by arranging your schedule around the Word instead of trying to make the Word fit into your busy schedule.
    a. Gloria read the Gospels and the book of Acts three times in 30 days, right after moving to Tulsa, while looking after her children and unpacking their house.

  b. Gloria got up at 5:30 and read until everyone got up and read during the children's naps.

  c. She accomplished this as well as painting and antiquing four pieces of furniture, finishing the accumulated ironing, and getting the house in order.

 5. Matthew 6:33: "Seek ye first the kingdom of God, and his righteousness; and all these things shall be added unto you."

  a. Give the Word time.

  b. Give the Word attention.

C. Psalm 34:10—Make God's Word Final Authority

 1. AMP: "The young lions lack food and suffer hunger, but they who seek (inquire of and require) the Lord [by right of their need and on the authority of His Word], none of them shall lack any beneficial thing."

 2. Romans 13:1 (AMP): "There is no authority except from God."

 3. Making God's Word final authority is believing what the Word says rather than believing people, Satan or circumstances.

  a. Believe you are what God's Word says you are.

  b. Believe you can do what God's Word says you can do.

  c. Believe you have what God's Word says you have.

 4. Matthew 8:7-10: "And Jesus saith unto him, I will come and heal him. The centurion answered and said, Lord, I am not worthy that thou shouldest come under my roof: but speak the word only, and my servant shall be healed. For I am a man under authority, having soldiers under me: and I say to this man, Go, and he goeth; and to another, Come, and he cometh; and to my servant, Do this, and he doeth it. When Jesus heard it, he marvelled, and said to them that followed, Verily I say unto you, I have not found so great faith, no, not in Israel."

 5. Make God's Word final authority by:

  a. Speaking the Word

  b. Meditating the Word

  c. Acting on the Word

  d. Making God's Word the first and last word in every situation of your life

DAYS OF PROSPERITY *Vol. 2*
Pastor George Pearsons

The Wealth of the Sinner
Day #93

A. Financial Inversion Shall Increase in These Days

Word from the Lord through Charles Capps, February 1, 1978

1. "Financial inversion shall increase in these days. For you see, it is My desire to move in the realm of your financial prosperity. But, release Me, saith the Lord, release Me that I may come in your behalf and move on your behalf.

2. "For yes, yes, yes, there shall be in this hour financial distress here and there. The economy shall go up and it will go down; but those who learn to walk in the Word, they shall see the prosperity of the Word come forth in this hour in a way that has not been seen by men in days past.

3. "Yes, there is coming a financial inversion in the world's system. It has been held in reservoirs of wicked men for days on end. But the end is nigh.

4. "Those reservoirs shall be tapped and shall be drained into the gospel of Jesus Christ. It shall be done, saith the Lord."
   a. A place where anything is collected in great amount
   b. A large or extra supply or stock; a reserve
   c. "Reservoirs are going to givers, the supporters of the gospel." —Gloria Copeland

5. "It shall be done in the time allotted and so shall it be that the word of the Lord shall come to pass that the wealth of the sinner is laid up for the just."

B. Proverbs 13:22—The Wealth of the Sinner

1. AMP: "A good man leaves an inheritance [of moral stability and goodness] to his children's children, and the wealth of the sinner [finds its way eventually] into the hands of the righteous, for whom it was laid up."

2. "A good person bequeaths his merits and wealth to his grandchildren. The sinner, however, leaves no inheritance, not even to his children; for his wealth is hidden away to be given to the righteous, as in the case of Haman, whose house and wealth were given to Mordechai." —From *Mishlei/Proverbs*

3. Esther 8:2 (NIV): "The king took off his signet ring, which he had reclaimed from Haman, and presented it to Mordecai. And Esther appointed him over Haman's estate."

4. Genesis 41:41-43 (NIV): "So Pharaoh said to Joseph, 'I hereby put you in charge of the whole land of Egypt.' Then Pharaoh took his signet ring from his finger and put it on Joseph's finger. He dressed him in robes of fine linen and put a gold chain around his neck. He had him ride in a chariot as his second-in-command, and men shouted before him, 'Make way!' Thus he put him in charge of the whole land of Egypt."

5. Daniel 2:48 (NIV): "Then the king placed Daniel in a high position and lavished many gifts on him. He made him ruler over the entire province of Babylon and placed him in charge of all its wise men."

C. Ecclesiastes 2:26—The Wealth of the Sinner

1. AMP: "For to the person who pleases Him God gives wisdom and knowledge and joy; but to the sinner He gives the work of gathering and heaping up, that he may give to one who pleases God."

2. NLT: "God gives wisdom, knowledge, and joy to those who please him. But if a sinner becomes wealthy, God takes the wealth away and gives it to those who please him."

3. Proverbs 22:22-23 (NIV-84): "Do not exploit the poor because they are poor and do not crush the needy in court, for the Lord will take up their case and will plunder those who plunder them."

4. Proverbs 6:30-31 (NIV): "People do not despise a thief if he steals to satisfy his hunger when he is starving. Yet if he is caught, he must pay sevenfold, though it costs him all the wealth of his house."

5. "Think about all of the sinners working for us. Let them heap up the money and transfer it to you." —From *The Kingdom of God—Days of Heaven on Earth* by Gloria Copeland

DAYS OF PROSPERITY *Vol. 2*
Pastor George Pearsons

The Wealth of Evil People
Day #94

A. Financial Inversion Shall Increase in These Days

Word from the Lord through Charles Capps, February 1, 1978

1. "Financial inversion shall increase in these days. For you see, it is My desire to move in the realm of your financial prosperity. But, release Me, saith the Lord, release Me that I may come in your behalf and move on your behalf.

2. "For yes, yes, yes, there shall be in this hour financial distress here and there. The economy shall go up and it will go down; but those who learn to walk in the Word, they shall see the prosperity of the Word come forth in this hour in a way that has not been seen by men in days past.

3. "Yes, there is coming a financial inversion in the world's system. It has been held in reservoirs of wicked men for days on end. But the end is nigh.

4. "Those reservoirs shall be tapped and shall be drained into the gospel of Jesus Christ. It shall be done, saith the Lord."
   a. A place where anything is collected in great amount
   b. A large or extra supply or stock; a reserve

5. "It shall be done in the time allotted and so shall it be that the word of the Lord shall come to pass that the wealth of the sinner is laid up for the just."

B. Job 27:16-19—The Wealth of Evil People

1. Verses16-17 (NLT): "Evil people may have piles of money and may store away mounds of clothing. But the righteous will wear that clothing, and the innocent will divide that money."

2. Verse 19 (NLT): "The wicked go to bed rich but wake to find that all their wealth is gone."
   a. "If you don't have it—demand it." —Gloria Copeland
   b. "A 'suddenly' that is going the wrong way" —Gloria Copeland
   c. "Overnight financial reversals" —Gloria Copeland

3. "What happens to evil people's money? Whether money is good or bad depends on who has the money. When the righteous have money, they do good things with it. When the wicked have money, they do bad things with it. And those bad things lead to death—many times at an early age. You can't look at the rich and wonder how they got their money. Money acquired by ill-gotten gain is not from God. You could be part of the

mafia and have lots of money—but you probably won't live out your full number of days. What happens to all of the 'ill-gotten gained' money? It goes right into the hands of the just." —From *True Prosperity* by Gloria Copeland

C. Proverbs 28:8—The Wealth of the Loan Shark
1. NIV-84: "He who increases his wealth by exorbitant interest amasses it for another, who will be kind to the poor."
2. AMP: "He who by charging excessive interest and who by unjust efforts to get gain increases his material possession gathers it for him [to spend] who is kind and generous to the poor."
3. Proverbs 14:31 (NIV): "Whoever oppresses the poor shows contempt for their Maker, but whoever is kind to the needy honors God."
4. Proverbs 19:17 (NLT): "If you help the poor, you are lending to the Lord—and he will repay you!"
5. "Think about the loan sharks, drug dealers and unjust gain. Think about the billions of dollars that God is going to vacuum in to the Kingdom. Start ministering to the poor if you want to get in on the end time transfer." —From *The Kingdom of God—Days of Heaven on Earth* by Gloria Copeland

DAYS OF PROSPERITY *Vol. 2*
Pastor George Pearsons

Here Comes the Wealth

Day #95

A. Financial Inversion Shall Increase in These Days
Word from the Lord through Charles Capps, February 1, 1978

1. "Financial inversion shall increase in these days. For you see, it is My desire to move in the realm of your financial prosperity. But, release Me, saith the Lord, release Me that I may come in your behalf and move on your behalf.

2. "For yes, yes, yes, there shall be in this hour financial distress here and there. The economy shall go up and it will go down; but those who learn to walk in the Word, they shall see the prosperity of the Word come forth in this hour in a way that has not been seen by men in days past.

3. "Yes, there is coming a financial inversion in the world's system. It has been held in reservoirs of wicked men for days on end. But the end is nigh.

4. "Those reservoirs shall be tapped and shall be drained into the gospel of Jesus Christ. It shall be done, saith the Lord."
   a. A place where anything is collected in great amount
   b. A large or extra supply or stock; a reserve

5. "It shall be done in the time allotted and so shall it be that the word of the Lord shall come to pass that the wealth of the sinner is laid up for the just."

B. Isaiah 60 (NLT)—Wealth Comes to Israel

1. Verses 5-7: "Your eyes will shine, and your heart will thrill with joy, for merchants from around the world will come to you. They will bring you the wealth of many lands. Vast caravans of camels will converge on you, the camels of Midian and Ephah. The people of Sheba will bring gold and frankincense and will come worshiping the Lord. The flocks of Kedar will be given to you, and the rams of Nebaioth will be brought for my altars. I will accept their offerings, and I will make my Temple glorious."

2. Verses 10-11: "Foreigners will come to rebuild your towns, and their kings will serve you. For though I have destroyed you in my anger, I will now have mercy on you through my grace. Your gates will stay open day and night to receive the wealth of many lands. The kings of the world will be led as captives in a victory procession."

3. Verse 13: "The glory of Lebanon will be yours—the forests of cypress, fir, and pine—to beautify my sanctuary. My Temple will be glorious!"

4. Verse 16: "Powerful kings and mighty nations will satisfy your every need, as though you were a child nursing at the breast of a queen. You will know at last that I, the Lord, am your Savior and your Redeemer, the Mighty One of Israel."
5. Isaiah 61:5: "And strangers shall stand and feed your flocks, and the sons of the alien shall be your plowmen and your vinedressers."

C. 1 Kings 10:10-12 (NIV)—Wealth Comes to Solomon
1. The Queen of Sheba was overwhelmed by Solomon's wisdom, prosperity and kingdom.
2. Verse 10a: "And she gave the king 120 talents [4.5 tons] of gold, large quantities of spices, and precious stones.
3. Verse 10b: "Never again were so many spices brought in as those the queen of Sheba gave to King Solomon."
4. Verse 11: "Hiram's ships brought gold from Ophir; and from there they brought great cargoes of almugwood and precious stones."
5. Verse 12: "The king used the almugwood to make supports for the temple of the Lord and for the royal palace, and to make harps and lyres for the musicians. So much almugwood has never been imported or seen since that day."

D. Matthew 2:7-11 (NLT)—Wealth Comes to Jesus
1. Verse 7: "Then Herod called for a private meeting with the wise men, and he learned from them the time when the star first appeared."
2. Verse 8: "Then he told them, 'Go to Bethlehem and search carefully for the child. And when you find him, come back and tell me so that I can go and worship him, too!'"
3. Verse 9: "After this interview the wise men went their way. And the star they had seen in the east guided them to Bethlehem. It went ahead of them and stopped over the place where the child was."
4. Verses 10-11: "When they saw the star, they were filled with joy! They entered the house and saw the child with his mother, Mary, and they bowed down and worshiped him. Then they opened their treasure chests and gave him gifts of gold, frankincense, and myrrh."
5. Psalm 72:10-11 (NIV-84): "The kings of Tarshish and of distant shores will bring tribute to him; the kings of Sheba and Seba will present him gifts. All kings will bow down to him and all nations will serve him."

International Church

DAYS OF PROSPERITY *Vol. 2*
Pastor George Pearsons

Get It 'To Go'!

Day #96

A. Financial Inversion Shall Increase in These Days
Word from the Lord through Charles Capps, February 1, 1978
  1. "Financial inversion shall increase in these days. For you see, it is My desire to move in the realm of your financial prosperity. But, release Me, saith the Lord, release Me that I may come in your behalf and move on your behalf.
  2. "For yes, yes, yes, there shall be in this hour financial distress here and there. The economy shall go up and it will go down; but those who learn to walk in the Word, they shall see the prosperity of the Word come forth in this hour in a way that has not been seen by men in days past.
  3. "Yes, there is coming a financial inversion in the world's system. It has been held in reservoirs of wicked men for days on end. But the end is nigh.
  4. "Those reservoirs shall be tapped and shall be drained into the gospel of Jesus Christ. It shall be done, saith the Lord."
       a. A place where anything is collected in great amount
       b. A large or extra supply or stock; a reserve
  5. "It shall be done in the time allotted and so shall it be that the word of the Lord shall come to pass that the wealth of the sinner is laid up for the just."

B. Transfer of Wealth From the Egyptians to the Children of Israel
  1. This is a prime example of massive wealth transfer.
       a. The Egyptians gave their wealth to the children of Israel on the way out of Egypt.
       b. They came out with silver and gold.
       c. The Egyptians said, "Take it and go and get out of our sight!"
  2. Exodus 3:20-22 (AMP): "So I will stretch out My hand and smite Egypt with all My wonders which I will do in it; and after that he will let you go. And I will give this people favor and respect in the sight of the Egyptians; and it shall be that when you go, you shall not go empty-handed. But every woman shall [insistently] solicit of her neighbor and of her that may be residing at her house jewels and articles of silver and gold, and garments, which you shall put on your sons and daughters; and you shall strip the Egyptians [of belongings due to you]."
  3. Exodus 12:35-36 (AMP): "The Israelites did according to the word of Moses; and they [urgently] asked of the Egyptians jewels of silver and of gold, and clothing. The Lord

gave the people favor in the sight of the Egyptians, so that they gave them what they asked. And they stripped the Egyptians [of those things]."

      a. Verse 36 (NIV): "They plundered the Egyptians."

      b. Verse 36 (MSG): "They picked those Egyptians clean."

4. Psalm 105:37 (AMP): "He brought [Israel] forth also with silver and gold, and there was not one feeble person among their tribes."

      a. *Feeble* (HEB)—There was not one pauper among their tribes.

      b. Pauper

            i. An extremely poor person

            ii. A person without any means of support

           iii. A destitute person who depends on aid from public welfare funds or charity

      c. *Tehillim* Commentary:

            i. Rabbi Eliezer the Great taught: The lowliest among the children of Israel brought ninety asses laden with silver and gold when he left Egypt.

            ii. The feeble man is one who became impoverished and stumbled from his original financial level. No Jew who left Egypt could be described as a pauper because all were enriched by the booty of their oppressors.

           iii. The pauper is a man whose health has deteriorated to the point that he stumbles unless he uses a cane. When the Jews left Egypt, a miracle occurred—not a single person amongst them was sick or debilitated.

      d. MSG: "He led Israel out, their arms filled with loot."

C. Deuteronomy 6:10-11—Wealth Transfer in the Promised Land

1. Great and goodly cities with they did not build

2. Houses they didn't fill, full of good things

3. Wells dug they didn't dig

4. Vineyards and olive trees which they didn't plant

5. Deuteronomy 6:3—It was a land that flowed with milk and honey.

EAGLE MOUNTAIN
International Church

DAYS OF PROSPERITY *Vol. 2*
Pastor George Pearsons

Transfer From the Enemy's Camp

Day #97

A. Financial Inversion Shall Increase in These Days

Word from the Lord through Charles Capps, February 1, 1978

1. "Financial inversion shall increase in these days. For you see, it is My desire to move in the realm of your financial prosperity. But, release Me, saith the Lord, release Me that I may come in your behalf and move on your behalf.

2. "For yes, yes, yes, there shall be in this hour financial distress here and there. The economy shall go up and it will go down; but those who learn to walk in the Word, they shall see the prosperity of the Word come forth in this hour in a way that has not been seen by men in days past.

3. "Yes, there is coming a financial inversion in the world's system. It has been held in reservoirs of wicked men for days on end. But the end is nigh.

4. "Those reservoirs shall be tapped and shall be drained into the gospel of Jesus Christ. It shall be done, saith the Lord."
   a. A place where anything is collected in great amount
   b. A large or extra supply or stock; a reserve

5. "It shall be done in the time allotted and so shall it be that the word of the Lord shall come to pass that the wealth of the sinner is laid up for the just."

B. 2 Kings 7:3-8—Wealth Transfer From the Enemy's Camp

1. Verses 3-4—The lepers decided to go to the Syrian camp.
2. Verse 5—No one was there.
3. Verse 6—The Lord created the noise of chariots.
4. Verse 7—The Syrians left everything in the camp.
5. Verse 8—The lepers ate, drank and took the gold, silver and clothes.

C. Confusion in the World of the Wicked

1. Word from the Lord through Charles Capps:

"So shall it be as it was in that day [speaking about the lepers in 2 Kings 7] that confusion shall come to the world of the wicked. For they have sought their own ways and have walked in their own purposes. They have gained and hoarded up and kept from the gospel that with which they have prospered.

"But, in the days to come, the days are changing and the ways are changing.

"It shall be so that confusion shall be on every hand. The monetary system shall be disturbed. Men shall look here and shall look there looking for an answer. But they shall not find it.

"So shall it be that in these that have come and spoiled the camp, shall the men in this day walk in the midst of confusions that shall be in the day in which you live. They shall believe for and receive the direction of the Lord. They shall flee their possessions. They shall flee it—drop it here and drop it there because they hear of that which is coming like the Syrians that fled from that camp who left their goods.

"They will release it and they will let it go.

"But as the Christians pick it up, it will not be so. [The Christians won't be confused.] Then, it will flourish and it will prosper."

2. "When there is confusion all around, there is clarity in the life of the believer."
    —Gloria Copeland
3. "We will pick up opportunities the world has missed because of all the confusion."
    —Gloria Copeland
4. "It will come to pass that you will see the Word of the Lord at work. And the power of God will be set in the earth in a day in which men will stand in awe. For the wealth of the sinner is laid up for the just. It is time, says the Lord, that it finds its way into the hands of the just. And so shall the gospel be preached throughout the land.

    "Walk in My precepts. For you shall hear with the ear a little at a time. And, I will reveal a little at a time. So shall you know that day that it will come. So, walk in My precepts and it will be done." —From *The Kingdom of God—Days of Heaven on Earth* by Gloria Copeland

D. 2 Chronicles 20:25-26 (AMP): "When Jehoshaphat and his people came to take the spoil, they found among them much cattle, goods, garments, and precious things which they took for themselves, more than they could carry away, so much they were three days in gathering the spoil. On the fourth day they assembled in the Valley of Beracah. There they blessed the Lord. So the name of the place is still called the Valley of Beracah [blessing]."

DAYS OF PROSPERITY *Vol. 2*
Pastor George Pearsons

Two Ways of Wealth Transfer

Day #98

A. Financial Inversion Shall Increase in These Days
Word from the Lord through Charles Capps, February 1, 1978

1. "Financial inversion shall increase in these days. For you see, it is My desire to move in the realm of your financial prosperity. But, release Me, saith the Lord, release Me that I may come in your behalf and move on your behalf.

2. "For yes, yes, yes, there shall be in this hour financial distress here and there. The economy shall go up and it will go down; but those who learn to walk in the Word, they shall see the prosperity of the Word come forth in this hour in a way that has not been seen by men in days past.

3. "Yes, there is coming a financial inversion in the world's system. It has been held in reservoirs of wicked men for days on end. But the end is nigh. Those reservoirs shall be tapped and shall be drained into the gospel of Jesus Christ. It shall be done, saith the Lord."
    a. A place where anything is collected in great amount
    b. A large or extra supply or stock; a reserve

4. "It shall be done in the time allotted and so shall it be that the word of the Lord shall come to pass that the wealth of the sinner is laid up for the just.

5. "Predominantly in two ways shall it be done in this hour:
    a. "Those who have hoarded up and stored because of the inspiration of the evil one and held the money from the gospel shall be converted and drawn into the Kingdom.
    b. "But many, many will not. They'll not heed the voice of the Word of God. They will turn aside to this and they will turn to that and they will walk in their own ways. But their ways will not work in this hour. It will dwindle and it will slip away as though it were in bags with holes in them. It will go here and it will go there and they will wonder why it is not working now. 'It worked in days past,' they will say."

B. Luke 19:1-10 (NIV)—The Conversion of Zacchaeus

1. Verses 1-2: "Jesus entered Jericho and was passing through. A man was there by the name of Zacchaeus; he was a chief tax collector and was wealthy."
2. Verses 3-4: "He wanted to see who Jesus was, but because he was short he could not see over the crowd. So he ran ahead and climbed a sycamore-fig tree to see him, since Jesus was coming that way."
3. Verses 5-6: "When Jesus reached the spot, he looked up and said to him, 'Zacchaeus, come down immediately. I must stay at your house today.' So he came down at once and welcomed him gladly."
4. Verses 7-8: "All the people saw this and began to mutter, 'He has gone to be the guest of a sinner.' But Zacchaeus stood up and said to the Lord, 'Look, Lord! Here and now I give half of my possessions to the poor, and if I have cheated anybody out of anything, I will pay back four times the amount.'"
5. Verses 9-10: "Jesus said to him, 'Today salvation has come to this house, because this man, too, is a son of Abraham. For the Son of Man came to seek and to save the lost.'"

C. Luke 12:13-21—A Rich Man's Wealth Transferred

1. Verses 13-14: "And one of the company said unto him, Master, speak to my brother, that he divide the inheritance with me. And he said unto him, Man, who made me a judge or a divider over you?"
2. Verse 15: "And he said unto them, Take heed, and beware of covetousness: for a man's life consisteth not in the abundance of the things which he possesseth."
3. Verses 16-17: "And he spake a parable unto them, saying, The ground of a certain rich man brought forth plentifully: And he thought within himself, saying, What shall I do, because I have no room where to bestow my fruits?"
4. Verses 18-19: "And he said, This will I do: I will pull down my barns, and build greater; and there will I bestow all my fruits and my goods. And I will say to my soul, Soul, thou hast much goods laid up for many years; take thine ease, eat, drink, and be merry."
5. Verses 20-21: "But God said unto him, Thou fool, this night thy soul shall be required of thee: then whose shall those things be, which thou hast provided? So is he that layeth up treasure for himself, and is not rich toward God."
   a. NIV: "Then who will get what you have prepared for yourself?"
   b. Psalm 39:6 (NIV-84): "He heaps up wealth, not knowing who will get it."
   c. Isaiah 10:1-3 (NIV): "Woe to those who make unjust laws, to those who issue oppressive decrees, to deprive the poor of their rights and withhold justice from the oppressed of my people, making widows their prey and robbing the fatherless. What will you do on the day of reckoning, when disaster comes from afar? To whom will you run for help? Where will you leave your riches?"
   d. Proverbs 13:22: "The wealth of the sinner is laid up for the just."
   e. Jeremiah 17:11: "As the partridge sitteth on eggs, and hatcheth them not; so he that getteth riches, and not by right, shall leave them in the midst of his days, and at his end shall be a fool."

D. 1 Timothy 6:9-10, 17-18—Surviving the Wealth

    1. Verses 9-10: "But they that will be rich fall into temptation and a snare, and into many foolish and hurtful lusts, which drown men in destruction and perdition. For the love of money is the root of all evil: which while some coveted after, they have erred from the faith, and pierced themselves through with many sorrows."

    2. Verses 17-18: "Charge them that are rich in this world, that they be not highminded, nor trust in uncertain riches, but in the living God, who giveth us richly all things to enjoy; that they do good, that they be rich in good works, ready to distribute, willing to communicate."

    3. We must be taught and trained how to handle wealth—or it will handle us.

    4. We survive the wealth by:

        a. Tithing

        b. Sowing

        c. Obeying

        d. Serving

    5. We must develop our "wealthability" (new word by Gloria Copeland).

EAGLE MOUNTAIN
International Church

DAYS OF PROSPERITY *Vol. 2*
Pastor George Pearsons

End Time Wealth Transfer

Day #99

A. Financial Inversion Shall Increase in These Days
Word from the Lord through Charles Capps, February 1, 1978
1. "Financial inversion shall increase in these days. For you see, it is My desire to move in the realm of your financial prosperity. But, release Me, saith the Lord, release Me that I may come on your behalf and move on your behalf.
2. "For yes, yes, yes, there shall be in this hour financial distress here and there. The economy shall go up and it will go down; but those who learn to walk in the Word, they shall see the prosperity of the Word come forth in this hour in a way that has not been seen by men in days past.
3. "Yes, there is coming a financial inversion in the world's system. It has been held in reservoirs of wicked men for days on end. But the end is nigh. Those reservoirs shall be tapped and shall be drained into the gospel of Jesus Christ. It shall be done, saith the Lord."
    a. A place where anything is collected in great amount
    b. A large or extra supply or stock; a reserve
4. "It shall be done in the time allotted and so shall it be that the word of the Lord shall come to pass that the wealth of the sinner is laid up for the just.
5. "Predominantly in two ways shall it be done in this hour:
    a. "Those who have hoarded up and stored because of the inspiration of the evil one and held the money from the gospel shall be converted and drawn into the Kingdom.
    b. "But many, many will not. They'll not heed the voice of the word of God. They will turn aside to this and they will turn to that and they will walk in their own ways. But their ways will not work in this hour. It will dwindle and it will slip away as though it were in bags with holes in them. It will go here and it will go there and they will wonder why it is not working now. 'It worked in days past,' they will say."

B. The Final Stage of Wealth Transfer
Word from the Lord through Kenneth Copeland, Branson Victory Campaign, March 8, 2012

"Now, this generation of people, the time in which you and I live, we are living in the most important time in God's schedule and what He has planned. You and I are living in "the" most important moment of time since the Day of Pentecost. Two thousand years of heaven going toward one specific event which is the catching away of the Body of Christ and glorification of His people. And, we are in it.

"Thank God for that early Church. Thank God for all of the great things that God has done over all this whole period of time. But, glory to God, we get to get in on it right here. This is the blowout! Do you understand?

"And I will give you a little bit of a preview here.

"Everything that Satan has accumulated in the way of property, wealth, influence—anything in this entire planet that he has his hands on and under his control, he stole it!

"Now, up until the ministry of Jesus on the earth from the time Adam committed treason before God—from that time until Jesus came into the earth, there were things that Satan did and accumulated. He did not have to steal because it had been put into his hands. And what he did and what he had, he got from Adam. Adam gave it to him. Don't you remember when Satan said to Jesus, 'Look at all of the kingdoms of this world. Bow down before me and I will give them to you. They have been given to me and I give it to whomsoever I will.' 'Now, Brother Copeland, he's [the devil is] a liar....'

"But, Jesus got it back! He took from him everything that he had taken from Adam. He took it back!

"The largest, most significant transfer of property, goods, wealth and people from the hands of the devil into the hands of God's people that are prepared to receive it—I am telling you the biggest transfer of property in the history of mankind has just begun and it is swinging into...it has moved over into its final stage, saith The LORD.

"And those who will listen to Me and follow Me and trust Me—those who I have taught My WORD and have given the authority to walk in these things, it is the most outstanding thing that human eyes have ever seen. And the time is now. Your time has come. Your hour has come. So rise and do those things by faith that you know to do and all that belongs to heaven will come into your hands for your joy."

C. James 5:1-8—You Have Heaped Treasure Together for the Last Days
Quotes from *Supernatural Wealth Transfer* by Bill Winston
1. "[God is] restoring the earth back into the hands of its rightful owners, as well as restoring the power or Blessing to govern it. Because of Adam's sin, the earth was not in the hands of God's family. Now, God is working His redemptive plan to get it all back...what I refer to as a *supernatural* transfer of wealth.
2. "As we get closer to our Lord's return, there is an invasion of the kingdom of heaven into this world—the imposing of God's will on the plans of the devil. Earthly systems, laws, rules, policies and values must now come in line with Heaven's order or Heaven's

Government, the Government of the Kingdom of God. Psalm 103:19 (ESV)... His kingdom rules over all.

3. "One of the major things coming in this hour is an *explosion of wealth* in the Body of Christ. Through divine favor, witty inventions and the grace of giving, we are at the season of the greatest *wealth transfer* in the history of this planet. There will be inventions that make the iPhone© seem like child's play.

4. "This is a prophetic time in history, the same as the "set-time" that triggered the release of the children of Israel from Egyptian bondage. This is a season when, what happened then is happening now. It is a set-time or a season which is the consummation of something pledged or promised by God. The reservoirs of the wicked will now be drained, and as the Babylonian system of the world fails, the system of the Kingdom of God will prevail.

5. "We are even going to see money supernaturally transfer into the bank accounts of the people of God. Why the transfer of wealth? Mainly for the advancing of the kingdom and bringing in the end-time harvest of souls. God needs the wealth in our hands to fulfill the call that is on our lives for this generation—to reclaim what Jesus redeemed."

D. Isaiah 53:12: "Therefore will I divide him a portion with the great, and he shall divide the spoil with the strong; because he hath poured out his soul unto death: and he was numbered with the transgressors; and he bare the sin of many, and made intercession for the transgressors."

EAGLE MOUNTAIN
International Church

DAYS OF PROSPERITY *Vol. 2*
Pastor George Pearsons

The Hundredfold Wealth Transfer

Day #100

A. Financial Inversion Shall Increase in These Days
Word from the Lord through Charles Capps, February 1, 1978

1. "Financial inversion shall increase in these days. For you see, it is My desire to move in the realm of your financial prosperity. But, release Me, saith the Lord, release Me that I may come in your behalf and move on your behalf.

2. "For yes, yes, yes, there shall be in this hour financial distress here and there. The economy shall go up and it will go down; but those who learn to walk in the Word, they shall see the prosperity of the Word come forth in this hour in a way that has not been seen by men in days past.

3. "Yes, there is coming a financial inversion in the world's system. It has been held in reservoirs of wicked men for days on end. But the end is nigh. Those reservoirs shall be tapped and shall be drained into the gospel of Jesus Christ. It shall be done, saith the Lord."
   a. A place where anything is collected in great amount
   b. A large or extra supply or stock; a reserve

4. "It shall be done in the time allotted and so shall it be that the word of the Lord shall come to pass that the wealth of the sinner is laid up for the just.

5. "Predominantly in two ways shall it be done in this hour:
   a. "Those who have hoarded up and stored because of the inspiration of the evil one and held the money from the gospel shall be converted and drawn into the Kingdom.
   b. "But many, many will not. They'll not heed the voice of the Word of God. They will turn aside to this and they will turn to that and they will walk in their own ways. But their ways will not work in this hour. It will dwindle and it will slip away as though it were in bags with holes in them. It will go here and it will go there and they will wonder why it is not working now. 'It worked in days past,' they will say.

6. "But it shall be, saith the Lord, that the word of the Lord shall rise within men—men of God of low esteem in the financial world—that shall claim the Word of God to be their very own and walk in the light of it as it has been set forth in the Word and give.

7. "They will begin to give small at first because that is all they have. But then it will increase, and through the hundredfold return, so shall it be that the reservoirs that have held the riches in days past, so shall it return to the hands of the giver. Because of the hundredfold return shall the reservoirs be lost from the wicked and turned to the gospel."

8. "For it shall be in this hour that you will see things that you have never dreamed come to pass. Oh, it will be strong at first in ways. Then, it will grow greater and greater until men will be astounded and the world will stand in awe because the ways of men have failed and the ways of God shall come forth."

B. Mark 10:28-30—The Hundredfold Return

Quotes from *God's Will Is Prosperity* by Gloria Copeland

1. "Peter began to say unto him, Lo, we have left all and have followed thee. And Jesus answered and said, Verily I say unto you, There is no man that hath left house, or brethren, or sisters, or father, or mother, or wife, or children, or lands, for my sake, and the gospel's, but he shall receive an hundredfold now in this time, houses, and brethren, and sisters, and mothers, and children, and lands, with persecutions; and in the world to come eternal life."

2. "How great the hundredfold return is: give $1 and receive 100!"

3. "Where in the natural world are you offered the return of 100 times your investment?"
   a. "If you double your money, you do well."
   b. "If you receive 10 times your investment, it is a marvelous deal."
   c. "But who talks in terms of receiving 100 times your investment?"

4. "After I let what the Word offers us in the hundredfold return become a reality to me, the Lord led me to continually give thanks for it every time I thought about it."
   a. "I would say, 'Thank You, Father, for the hundredfold return offered in Your Word.'"
   b. "It is such a generous return and it belongs to me."

5. "I would say any faith words of praise that came into my spirit in regard to continually thanking God for the hundredfold return."
   a. "This thanksgiving kept my faith active and operative to receive."
   b. "Continually confessing the hundredfold return causes the seed of Mark 10:29-30 to grow."

C. Genesis 26:12-14—Transfer of Wealth to Isaac

1. Verses 12-14 (MSG): "Isaac planted crops in that land and took in a huge harvest. God blessed him. The man got richer and richer by the day until he was very wealthy. He accumulated flocks and herds and many, many servants, so much so that the Philistines began to envy him."

2. The Philistines envied him because their wealth was being transferred to Isaac.

3. "Through the hundredfold return, so shall it be that the reservoirs that have held the riches in days past, so shall it return to the hands of the giver. Because of the hundredfold return shall the reservoirs be lost from the wicked and turned to the gospel." —From *God's Will Is Prosperity* by Gloria Copeland

4. Continually confess, "The hundredfold return is working for me."
5. Then, believe for and receive a continual flow of the wealth of the world being transferred into your life.

"Under the curse, you diminish. Things flow away from you.
Under THE BLESSING, you increase. Things flow into you."

—Gloria Copeland